Olivier Dwek in the light of modernity

Olivier Dwek in the light of modernity

Philip Jodidio

Rizzoli
NEW YORK
New York · Paris · London · Milan

To Harry & Théodora

“Dreams are my source, my shepherd’s crook, my island.
At the edge of my window, a feather.
Deep inside a shell, the sea.
At the foot of a cliff, marcasite.
In the slightest happiness, good fortune…
Beauty is everywhere, in the course of sharing and in encounters.
My meeting with Olivier goes back to his childhood, and since then his passion has come a long way…
Elegant and refined, his idea of luxury is the emergence of sobriety in architecture that allows natural light to turn within it.
The best place is where time is suspended,
where the magic happens…”

Ado Chale

Bathed in the light of modernity

Unlike some architects who tend to put forward every project they complete, Olivier Dwek has developed a culture of discretion, based partially on the desires of his clients, who are often major art and design collectors. But his discretion is also a personal preference, a desire surely to concentrate all his efforts and time on his projects rather than on self-promotion. Like some other high-level architect-designers, such as Thierry Despont and Peter Marino in New York, Jacques Grange in Paris, or John Pawson in London, Dwek has a broad-ranging cosmopolitan knowledge of art, furniture design, and architecture. He has an innate ability to combine periods and works in unexpected yet somehow fully compatible ways—placing paintings by Jean-Michel Basquiat or Christopher Wool near furniture by Charlotte Perriand or George Nakashima. When it comes to his own tastes, Dwek admits that one of his favorite cultural buildings is Renzo Piano's Beyeler Foundation (Riehen, Switzerland, 1997). This thoroughly modern building has a distinct feeling of natural materiality rendered by its façades in Patagonian porphyry or its light wood floors, and above all its abundant but carefully controlled natural light. In his own work, Olivier Dwek has made a point of providing for natural light, through skylights or windows, but most often in ways that privilege the art, in the broadest sense, that inhabits his realizations. Another cultural institution that the architect cites is the Louisiana Museum of Modern Art (Humlebaek, Denmark, 1958). The Louisiana Museum is known, of course, for its groundbreaking exhibitions but also for its 1950s Modernist architecture by Jørgen Bo and Vilhlem Wohlert. Dwek states: "One has to try to set aside direct influences so that they don't wind up becoming parasitical. Any creative person has an artistic father or mother, and it is important to take some distance from them. I admit it, Ludwig Mies van der Rohe, Richard Meier, and John Pawson all had a certain influence on me. Like them, I like what is simple or pure, but then, I like to add unexpected elements that will create surprises or add an extra dimension."[1] Dwek's references indicate clearly that alongside his interest in art and design, he considers himself to be first and foremost an architect.

The Artist's Eye

Born in Brussels, Olivier Dwek explains that in the period before he went to university he was fascinated by the history of art. "When I was about 17 or 18 years old," he says, "I read the biographies of as many 19th-century, Impressionist, or Post-Impressionist artists as I could find. At the same time, I worked on drawings of nudes at the Académie des Beaux-Arts in Brussels. It was drawing that attracted me, and I think that drawing also led me to architecture. And so I went on to actually study architecture at the Institut Victor Horta." At the time, Belgium still considered architecture to be an artistic form of expression and not grounds for study in the university system per se. As is the case in France, for example, the "Beaux-Arts" included architecture as one of its disciplines, more precisely in the structure of the Institut Victor Horta in Brussels. Despite his decision to study at Horta (1990–95), Dwek says today: "I must admit that I was not 100% convinced that I actually wanted to be an architect at that time. I realized, though, that I wanted to be an actor in the world of creativity and not a spectator." Although he makes this distinction about his education and his life decisions, Olivier Dwek has,

Olivier Dwek photographed by Jarmo Pohjaniemi.

1. Where not otherwise indicated, all quotes by Olivier Dwek are from conversations with the author, April 1 and 8, 2020.

in fact, found a very good way to put his interest in art to very practical use, counseling his clients and working with them to place artworks and design to their best advantage. The fact that he does so with an extensive knowledge of modern and contemporary forms of art and design, the fact that he does so with an "eye" that understands and fashions space and the relation between volumes and objects, makes Olivier Dwek an exceptional figure.

The Belgian system requires graduates to spend two years working in an architectural office before they are allowed to sign plans on their own. Olivier Dwek undertook this process with a relatively large office, Art & Build Architect in Brussels (1995–96), but his goal was not to work his way up through the ranks spending time on projects that were not his own. "Once I had completed my studies," he says, "I felt a real need to carry out my own projects, and to have my own office. When I was 28, Louis Vuitton asked me directly to work on their Brussels store. The building already existed, but we kept only the late 19th-century façades as required by the city. The entire interior of the building was gutted and rebuilt. This task was more complex than building a new structure. Louis Vuitton had their own style for the actual decoration of the store—I created the spaces and volumes, the real architecture of the store. I fully appreciate how daring they were to hire such a young architect for such a prestigious commission." Despite being circumscribed by the walls of an existing building, Dwek's first project can be described as a work of pure architecture, an articulation of volumes and light that the client then used as they saw fit. His success in working with a client as prestigious as Louis Vuitton before he turned 30 makes it clear that Olivier Dwek had a kind of innate understanding of the complexities of architecture, one that did not have to be honed by years of experience in a subalternate role. Demanding work for an international brand put him immediately on a track where precision and high-quality materials and realization were the rule rather than the exception. Convinced on this basis of his ability to generate further new commissions, Olivier Dwek founded his own office in Brussels in 2000.

Combining the Old and the New

In 2006, the Walloon Region of Belgium selected him to convert the former industrial site of the well-known firearms manufacturer Fabrique Nationale Herstal in Liege into a residential, commercial, and cultural complex. In that instance Dwek was asked to create 350 modular homes, and he responded by designing an ecologically responsible 105,000-square-meter complex built on the 200-meter-long concrete slabs of the upper floor of the former sheds. The interesting point here is that the industrial heritage of the site was conserved at the same time as the complex was repurposed in a thoroughly modern way. Olivier Dwek comments: "The Fabrique Nationale is one of the most significant industrial sites in Belgium, together with Tour & Taxis in Brussels. We were chosen in an invited competition to undertake the complete rehabilitation of the site. There were residences, retail space, the museum of the Fabrique Nationale, a hotel, offices, something like a piece of the city within the city. In my mind, this enormous project was like a horizontal skyscraper." The project, which began construction in 2017, has not been completed, for reasons entirely unrelated to Dwek's scheme. His design, on the contrary, offered one of the few ways to actually make use of such a vast industrial site in an intelligent and coherent way. This was not a "jewel" in the sense of the Louis Vuitton store; it was an overt combination of the old and the new, of the industrial and the contemporary—a contrast that Dwek has frequently mastered in his work since that time.

Louis Vuitton shop in Brussels. A 19th-century building entirely redesigned by Olivier Dwek.

LOUIS VUITTON
LOUIS VUITTON
VUITTON

Although he continues to work on large-scale architectural projects, Olivier Dwek has made his reputation in recent years with residences and smaller cultural venues where his full talents—not only as an architect, but also as a person with a sensitive and broad understanding of art and design—have been fully implemented. "My involvement in projects that give a larger place to art and design was a question of circumstances and clients," he states. "I worked on pure architecture, but also on interior architecture in a self-taught way from the very beginning. I had no specific background in interior work. I feel that the only difference between architecture, interior architecture, or even design is essentially one of scale and proportions. My philosophy and my way of drawing in these instances are very similar."

From an Armchair to a House

Olivier Dwek continues to express the natural curiosity that led him to read everything he could about artists when he was younger. An important component of his more recent work has been the placement and sometimes the acquisition of significant works of modern design. "I became more interested in furniture and decorative arts in about 2000," he says. "I found myself attracted in a very natural way to 20th-century furniture, which we might call Modernist or mid-century, and I started to collect objects myself around that time. Whenever I was able to, I bought a Danish piece from the 1950s, for example. I find it fascinating to live with furniture like this but also to contemplate and analyze it. I express my interest for these objects in a self-instructed way, but I do think that my approach serves to broaden my horizons." Although it might be unexpected for an architect to delve so deeply into art and design, Olivier Dwek gives a convincing explanation for his own methods; one that does relate to architecture. "These pieces are often quite close to architecture albeit on a different scale," he says. "A *bahut* cabinet designed by Jean Prouvé in 1950 is not that far from some of the residential projects of Le Corbusier in its form, for example. Take an *Easy* armchair (1955) by Pierre Jeanneret and look at the central pillars of Jean Prouvé's 6x9 Demountable House (1944–45): they both rely on wooden braces of a similar form. In a formal sense, what holds up a chair also holds up a house." In explaining the innate relation that he sees between design and architecture in the work of figures such as Oscar Niemeyer, Le Corbusier, Charlotte Perriand, Pierre Jeanneret, and Jean Prouvé, Olivier Dwek also further makes his point about scale. He says that he sees no absolute distinction between a large building and a smaller project; he draws them both with the same spirit of harmony, natural light, and carefully selected materials. If a piece of furniture can have fundamental architectural qualities, so, too, can architecture (interior or exterior) take on the precision and equilibrium of the best works of object design.

Many architects are interested in art or design, but few succeed as frequently as Olivier Dwek does in designing homes or cultural locations that are as full of pieces of both that are at the highest level. He explains: "Bit by bit, I have been able to communicate my passion for design furniture to my clients, sometimes by encouraging art collectors to begin their own collection of furniture, or by guiding others to make the right choices. I would also add contemporary and modern ceramics as another of my areas of interest. There are numerous Japanese or American ceramists, for example, who have shown real evolution and change since the beginning of the 21st century, and I do advise my clients to discover such objects." Olivier Dwek, indeed, seems most at ease in environments in which architecture is one element of a broader composition in which art and design have a full place. Rather, too, his desire to place art quite

Velin chairs by Christian Liaigre, 1998; dining table by Ado Chale, 2007; bookcase by Obumex, 2006; pair of wall sconces by Jules Wabbes, ca. 1960.
On the table: *Grand Bassin* by Jean Girel, 2011.

Opposite
Oxidized bronze, patinated entrance door, made up of contiguous rectangular sections, designed by Olivier Dwek, 2006.

Above
Natural stone façades made up of contiguous rectangular sections, designed by Olivier Dwek; gray thermo-painted aluminum doorframes; natural stone terrace, 2006.

literally in the best light possible is one factor that leads him to bring plenty of natural light into his spaces, either through skylights or ample glazed walls for the more modern buildings or the ones designed by him. The architect imagines a building, visualizes space, turning it and molding it in his mind before committing it to paper and then transforming it into stone and steel. Dwek clearly applies a very similar logic to the placement of paintings or furniture in his spaces. An object, especially an exceptional one, has a soul and a presence that he feels. Placement, in natural light or within a volume, is ultimately a matter of taste and discernment, of respect for architecture, art, and design at the same level. Having an "eye" for these things is rare. Many talented architects go no further than to imagine empty buildings; few seek to fully animate and occupy their own creations, perhaps preferring to consider that the only real art is architecture. Figures that Olivier Dwek admires, such as Richard Meier or John Pawson, are known for wanting to photograph and even inaugurate some buildings empty. They use light to fill their architecture—so does Dwek. The Belgian also avoids strictly repetitive, grid-driven designs and materials. His signature is his taste, his "eye" more than any definable and frequently recycled style.

Architect and Curator

Speaking in particular of his work on the Seaflower Residence (p. 183), Olivier Dwek says: "Curator, decorator, architect, what I do is a kind of hybrid mixture of these disciplines." He goes on to explain: "I would say today that my knowledge of art remains greater than my knowledge of architecture. This allows me to have dialogues and even a certain complicity with my clients, who are often collectors of art and design." Along the same lines, Dwek has stated that he finds that there is no barrier between architecture and interior design: "When I am working on architecture, I have my pencil and my drawing paper. Drawing everything comes naturally to me. In all cases, it is a matter of proportions, of voids, of materials, and of functions. Only the scale varies."[2] Further to this point, Olivier Dwek says: "Architecture and interior design flow from the same philosophy of architecture and should be defined in terms of continuity. The interior cannot be the opposite of the exterior. Every element, even the materials chosen, must be responsive to each other. Take the example of the Silver House (p. 103): when the full-height glazing is open, there are patios and interior spaces. Are you in a living room or on a covered terrace? I believe in a form of architectural continuity that erases the distinction between interior and exterior."[3] Although Knokke-le-Zoute does not benefit from the Mediterranean climate of the Silver House, for the Seaflower apartment (p. 183) Dwek has designed a space in a building originally created by the Belgian architect Marc Corbiau in 1980. Knokke-le-Zoute is, of course, a seaside resort and this apartment building is in the dunes overlooking the North Sea. And so here, too, broad terraces and views bring the exterior into the apartment and make its interior one with the natural environment. A historic work by Donald Judd ("stack," 1965) was placed on a wall by Dwek so that, at the correct angle, it looks as though it is literally floating on the sea. Indeed, each piece, even a specially designed free-form rug, participates in a composition of architecture, art, and light.

Intemporal Design

Clearly Olivier Dwek is as much at ease with 19th-century industrial buildings as he is with the most contemporary art. He says: "I am seeking to design in a way that is intemporal. When I look at photos of my older projects, I say to myself that they are difficult to date and that amuses me. I am convinced that when one designs pure, clean things and that when no gesture is gratuitous, the result will be perennial. It is gratuitous gestures that condemn designs to age rapidly."[4]

This attitude also surely applies to his taste in modern furniture, which runs to the works of figures such as Jean Prouvé, a metalworker, architect, and engineer who actively intersected industrial design and modern living, or the Belgian Ado Chale (b. 1928), who is known for such pieces as a table made with a slab of petrified wood on a lacquered black steel base (ca. 1965).

Dwek does make a distinction between some of his favorite designers, like the American George Nakashima (1905–90), of whom he says: "He was a visionary with an ecological philosophy well before that became so popular. In a structural and formal sense, Nakashima's furniture is architectural." Ado Chale is, however, a different case, one that has a special place in the life of Olivier Dwek. "I have known Ado since I was a child," he explains. "I visited his atelier in Brussels with my parents when I was about five years old. My parents had many of his objects, so his world was one with which I was familiar. He is more of a poet, a creator, even an alchemist I would say than others who have a method that I would relate to architecture."

When he builds entirely new structures, such as the Silver House on Zante Island (p. 103), Olivier Dwek shows a talent for using the strict lines of modern and contemporary architecture in a way that permits the building to be in full communion with its spectacular natural setting. He succeeds in being at once modest and spectacular in his adroit composition of voids and solids, his contrasts of transparency and opacity. He references traditional Cycladic and Ionian Greek architecture and carves out views that can make a visitor understand how the Greek rocks, sky, and sea of Greece gave birth to modern civilization. And somehow, in this setting, a painting by Jean-Michel Basquiat is very much at home. Like many truly creative people, architects, artists, or designers, Dwek sees natural historical and visual links between periods. Early modern furniture is placed with natural ease in his carefully designed volumes, be they of earlier origin or fully contemporary, be they initially industrial or, on the contrary, urban and sophisticated. Contemporary art, too, stands out and can be appreciated most often in natural light, because Dwek's designs are quite literally meant to privilege art.

Past and Present, Inside and Out

Olivier Dwek says he is passionate about his work, but he follows a particular path, perhaps advancing through his own proudly self-taught interests in the various dimensions of architecture, art, and design. He states: "It is the artistic quality, the philosophy, the materials, and finally the atmosphere that interests me more than the sheer size of a project. We are above all architects, however, not decorators." Of course, his first major project, the Louis Vuitton building in Brussels, concerned the complete reconstruction of an interior volume, and Dwek went on from there to take on a 105,000-square-meter mixed-use complex, commencing his career with rather solid, essentially architectural works. The projects published in this volume are for the most part on a more intimate scale and show both his aptitude for designing interior volumes and also for entire structures, such as the houses in Greece, the Dominican Republic, or Belgium. Olivier Dwek, though, insists that this palette of realizations does not fully explain or show the range of his interests. He has been involved in ongoing projects in Mumbai that concern a 45-story tower, for which he will design the interiors, and a smaller (15-story) structure that will serve as the headquarters of a major property developer who was cited the best in his profession in India by CNN in 2020.

Following pages
The imposing and sheltering architecture of the Zeelied Residence, built in 2016 on the Belgian coast. The bay window and terraces look over the sand dunes. *Neutra* armchair by Vincent Van Duysen, 2008; ceramic by Takayuki Sakiyama, 2015; stools by Charlotte Perriand, ca. 1950–60

2. Olivier Dwek quoted in *Artravel* at http://www.artravelmagazine.com/olivier-dwek/ accessed April 4, 2020.
3. Olivier Dwek quoted in *Be Perfect*, summer 2019 at https://issuu.com/beperfectmagazine/docs/be_perfect_10-chemin_de_fer-forweb accessed April 4, 2020.
4. Olivier Dwek quoted in *Artravel* at http://www.artravelmagazine.com/olivier-dwek/ accessed April 4, 2020.

Though he prefers not to publish these unfinished works, it may suffice to say, as he does, that "there is an experimental and creative element in the smaller tower. I think that Cubism has had some influence on the design." Its irregular piled form creates varied openings and at once gives an impression of solidity and of being stacked, almost like a childhood game of wooden blocks. As he did in his Greek houses, the architect alternates solid volumes and openings in an intelligent and carefully orchestrated manner. There is something of the Modernist compositions of the De Stijl movement—Gerrit Rietveld's Schröder House (Utrecht, 1924)—albeit in a more vertical register. Here, as in the use of a large green marble wall in his recent New Hope Collection building (p. 49), Dwek makes a discreet nod to the early giants of modern architecture, in their sober, artful, geometric compositions. Indeed, Mies van der Rohe's Barcelona Pavilion (Spain, 1929) incarnates another area of interest for Dwek, a daring integration of interior and exterior. Of course, the climate of the Ionian islands makes this kind of integration easier than that of Brussels, but understanding his deep attachment to natural light, which in a sense dissolves the barriers between inside and outside, is one key to grasping the quality and interest of the work of Olivier Dwek.

In addition, his careful attention to materials, colors, surfaces, and the juxtaposition of periods and styles—admitting elements of early industrial architecture to a place for the display of contemporary art—offer more insight to his work. This can be clearly seen in the CAB (p. 73), N.E.S.T. (p. 141), and New Hope Collection (p. 49) buildings. Where other architects, even very talented ones, see their task as completing empty volumes, Olivier Dwek succeeds in inhabiting his spaces with light, but also with objects and works of art. His own art is one of the orchestration of apparently different elements to create an aesthetic whole. Tellingly, he states: "I prefer to seek inspiration and sources of thought in other areas of artistic expression than in architecture itself." It may be in explaining his reasoning in going beyond empty volumes that Dwek most clearly underlines the interest of his approach and his work. "The insistence on modern furniture in my projects is very much of my doing," he says. "I would say that my DNA as an architect comes from early 20th-century Modernism. I would even dare to say that my aesthetic and architectural ancestors are the modern architects who made themselves known in the 1920s. I would concede that there is some nostalgia, even some romanticism, in these choices. In modern furniture, there is a real soul, a constructive discernment. Nakashima shows a true philosophical intelligence in his work. He is a visionary from the past who saw the future. I love art that dates from the end of the 19th century onward, when photography liberated art. Most of my clients collect contemporary art. I like a good collection of contemporary art—it is necessary to live in one's own time. I like the dialogue between periods. My clients do trust my eye and they often ask me to select and place their works in the spaces that I design. In those cases, I act rather like a curator."

Bring in the Light

Olivier Dwek is an architect, but he is more than that—he is a person who sees and understands space and light, who knows how to look at a piece of furniture and to admire it as much as he might a building by Mies van der Rohe. Although he is young, he was educated in a system that valued drawing, and, as he says, drawing has been the link in his life between art and architecture. Just as he has done in terms of disciplines, combining the work of architecture, interior design, and artistic curation, Dwek dissolves barriers between periods, between forms of expression, and finally, where circumstances permit, between interior and exterior.

The Zeelied Residence, seen from outside.

This aspect of his work is most apparent in his Greek houses (pp. 25, 103), or in a different way in Neuilly-sur-Seine (p. 83) and Knokke-le-Zoute (p. 183). Even where closed walls are the rule, he invites natural light in. Much as Japanese architects, like Tadao Ando, consider a shower of natural light or a breeze as being a real, tangible presence of nature in their buildings, Olivier Dwek includes daylight in all his work; light that unites interior and exterior and calls on our most basic feelings and instincts. Where his architecture approaches its purest and actually most geometric form, for example in the Silver House (p. 103), the real protagonist of the design is not so much his building as it is views of the sky and the sea, into which he inserts works of art. White and geometric, the architecture opens to the outside, to nature, to carefully planned views. Of course it contrasts with the rocky site, but Dwek here creates a place to live in communion not only with nature—with the blue of the sea and sky, with the strong light of the Mediterranean—but in aesthetic harmony and knowledge of the value of modernity. Greece is often seen as a cradle of Western civilization, and Olivier Dwek dares to draw a line between its ancient roots, its more recent white Ionian and Cycladic iterations, and the present. Dissolving barriers between periods and forms of expression, he dares not to put himself forward but, instead, to invite the light in. He takes in the influences of Mies or Meier, Prouvé or Chale, and does not fear that a work by Charlotte Perriand or Jean-Michel Basquiat may draw more attention than his subtle volumetric compositions. He is there, on the contrary, to permit the art to be placed in a privileged position, or to make visible a link between a 19th-century industrial building and contemporary forms and sensibilities. He is there not to create an artificial utopia, but to make spaces bathed in the light of modernity.

White Snow Dwarf (Dopey #2) artwork by Paul McCarthy, 2012; *Mother & Son* artwork by Louise Bourgeois, 2007; ceramics by Kristin McKirdy, 2015; *Pink and White Cloud* and *Turquoise and White Cloud* ceramics by Bente Skjøttgaard, 2014; *5005* coffee table by Paul Frankl, ca. 1948; sideboard by Jean Prouvé, ca. 1950; *Visiteur* armchair by Jean Prouvé, ca. 1948; *Standard* chair by Jean Prouvé, ca. 1950; *Swing-Jib* lamp by Jean Prouvé, ca. 1947.

Australian House

For his second house on the Ionian Island of Zante, Olivier Dwek was immediately seduced by the spectacular views from a site situated between the mountains and the sea. The sun, the wind, and the blue of the sky and sea guided him to orient the house toward the views and to nearly abolish the distinction between indoors and out with sliding glass walls. Here, as in the earlier Silver House (p. 103), his first creation on the island, he references the artist Yves Klein's fascination with the color blue—here the blue of the sea and the sky, coupled with white architecture that echoes local traditions. Built near the ruins of an old mill, the 250-square-meter house is located at the northern point of Zante, within sight of Cephalonia. Dwek has again called on a rigorous geometric vocabulary, coupled with carefully placed openings that make it clear that the real point of this house is the view. "The idea," says Olivier Dwek, "is not to dominate nature. On the contrary, the house should almost disappear. One could almost speak of 'non-architecture' where the interiors are concerned because of the way they put forward the view and dissolve the barriers between the exterior and the covered spaces." An outdoor jacuzzi and an infinity pool facing the sea affirm the outdoor life that the Greek climate encourages. Inside, the walls are white and the light-gray stone floors continue into the outdoor space. The interiors are, however, all the more remarkable because the architect was able to make a selection of 20th-century design furniture that includes pieces by the Japanese-American George Nakashima, the French designers Charlotte Perriand and Jean Prouvé, and the Belgian Ado Chale. "This furniture has a real soul," says Dwek, "a history and a character, and it contrasts in a beautiful way with the pristine architecture of the house, and, finally, gives it personality."

Cube chairs by Gunnar Aagaard Andersen, 1980; *EKC24* lounge chair by Poul Kjaerholm, 1965; *EKC62* side table by Poul Kjaerholm, 1968; *S.C.A.L.* daybed by Jean Prouvé, 1954.

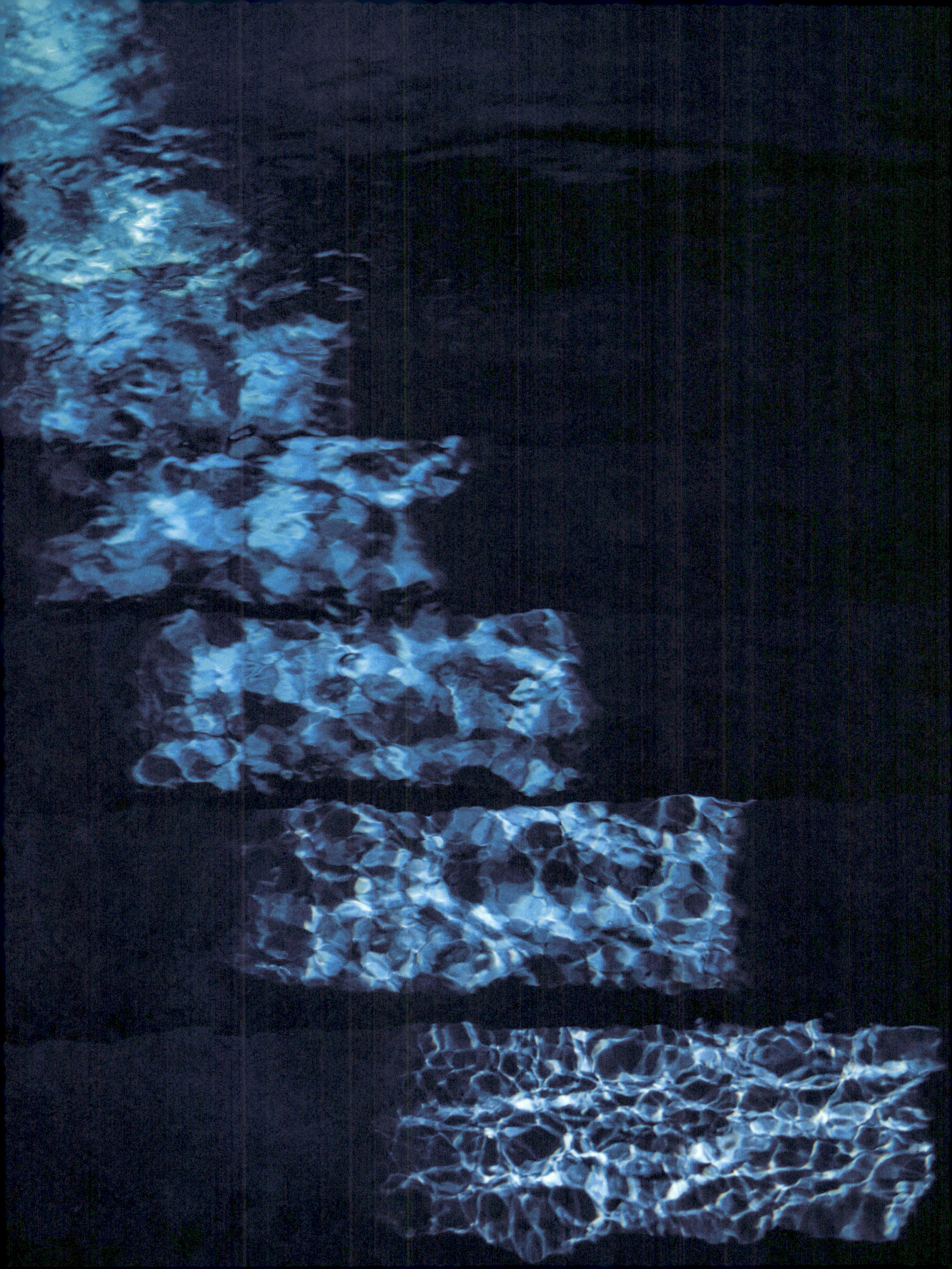

Opposite and above
Stools by Charlotte Perriand, ca. 1950–60; *Clam* chair by Philip Arctander, ca. 1940; *Grass-Seated* chairs by George Nakashima, ca. 1950; *PH5/3* floor lamp by Poul Henningsen, ca. 1930; *Son of Bozo* artwork by George Condo, 2009; *Conoid* dining table by George Nakashima, 1971.
On the table: ceramics by Tony Marsh, 2015; ceramic by Yoshiro Kimura, 2015.

Following pages
Banana sofa by Otto Schultz, ca. 1950; *Minguren II* side table by George Nakashima, ca. 1965; *Goutte d'eau* table by Ado Chale, ca. 1970; *PK80* daybed by Poul Kjaerholm, ca. 1950; stools by Charlotte Perriand, ca. 1950–60.
On the table: artwork by Ib Geertsen, 1950; *White Cloud* ceramic by Bente Skjøttgaard, 2017.

Opposite
Forme Libre table by Charlotte Perriand, ca. 1960; *Bridge Director* armchair by Jean Prouvé, ca. 1950.
On the table: *PH4/3* table lamps by Poul Henningsen, ca. 1930.

Following pages
Table Bench by Finn Juhl, ca. 1955; *Spin* artwork by Ritsue Mishima, 2017; *S.C.A.L.* daybed by Jean Prouvé, 1954.

New Hope Collection

Located in the Brussels area of Saint-Gilles, this industrial brick building was erected in two stages in 1890 (garage) and 1896 (small attached building) in what was described as an "eclectic" style.[1] Rue Américaine, where it is situated, runs between Ixelles and Saint-Gilles, and the site is across the street from the 1901 house and atelier of Victor Horta (1861–1947), the Art Nouveau Belgian architect and designer. Now the Horta Museum, that house is on the UNESCO World Heritage List together with three other Horta town houses. Because of the proximity of the Horta house, authorities required that the visible exterior surfaces and volumes of the New Hope Collection not be otherwise substantially altered, but no such conditions were posed for the interior, which was completely rebuilt by Olivier Dwek. The client for Dwek's 550-square-meter project was a collector of mid-century American and Scandinavian furniture. Thanks to Dwek's work, important pieces from the client's collection now echo works from the Charles Riva collection and important pieces from the French modern design collections of Daniel and David Lebard. Inside the relatively minimal, white-and-black space, "21st-century-style" skylights are underpinned by black steel crossbeams and columns. A thick, top-lit, 42-square-meter Italian green marble wall neighbors the entrance in a gesture that brings to mind the walls in the Ludwig Mies van der Rohe's Barcelona Pavilion (Spain, 1929). Aside from the entrance, the ground floor includes a terrace and seating areas, with groups of furniture by Ado Chale, Paul Evans, Jean Royère, Alexandre Noll, George Nakashima, Jules Wabbes, and Oscar Niemeyer. New Hope, Pennsylvania, is the location of Nakashima's home, studio, and workshop and thus the source of the name of the collection. An opening offers a view of the basement floor, which has further exhibition areas and storage spaces for large- and small-format artworks. A rooftop terrace and office occupy the top level. Here, as in other projects, Olivier Dwek shows his deft capacity to update old buildings while allowing them to retain much of their original flavor—the whole in an atmosphere that is particularly well suited to the display of contemporary and modern art and design.

1. See http://www.irismonument.be/fr/object/504 accessed March 30, 2020.

Ours polaire armchair and sofa by Jean Royère, 1947; *Alta* lounge chair by Oscar Niemeyer, 1972; *Two Guys Twice* by Richard Prince, 2001–02; *Untitled Sculpture – (Gong), Bally, PA* artwork by Harry Bertoia, ca. 1960; *Flaque* coffee table by Jean Royère, 1960; carpet by Maurice Pré, 1947.
On the table: *Chardons* candlestick by Hubert Le Gall, 2018.

UMB GUYS GO BEAR HUNTING
SEE A SIGN SAYING BEAR LEF
HEY WENT HOME. TWO DUMB
GO BEAR HUNTING. THEY SEE
SAYING BEAR LEFT, SO THEY
HOME.
Prince / Picasso

Above
Hanging wall cabinet by George Nakashima, ca. 1965; ceramic bottles by Suzanne Ramié, 1952 and 1965; *Pansue*, *Figue*, *Boule Ovoïde*, and *Boule* ceramics by Jacques and Dani Ruelland, 1960.

Opposite
Lightning vase by Marc Du Plantier, 1940; ceramics by Valérie Hermans, 2012.

Previous pages
Boomerang desk by Jules Wabbes, 1957; *MR 10* chairs by Ludwig Mies van der Rohe, 1927; *Lamp* painting by Philip Guston, 1979; hanging wall shelf by George Nakashima, ca. 1960; ceramic by Georges Jouve, 1955; ceramic by André Borderie, ca. 1960.
On the desk: *Babel* ceramic by Turi Heisselberg Pedersen, 2019; box by Paul Evans, ca. 1970.

Opposite
Wall sconce by Jules Wabbes, 1969; *Zombie* armchair by Roger Tallon, 1967.
In the background: the Horta Museum, former home and workshop of Victor Horta, Belgian Art Nouveau architect. It was inscribed on the UNESCO World Heritage List in 2000.

TEXAS

Previous pages
Left: *Texas* artwork by Ed Ruscha, 1962; cabinet by Paul Evans, 1970.
On the cabinet: *Black Botanica 1* ceramic by Helle Damkjaer, 2019; *Ensemble de trois Arbres* ceramics by Jacques and Dani Ruelland, ca. 1970–80.
Right: *Automatic Oracle* artwork by Robert Motherwell, 1989; *Egyptian* stools by Ole Wanscher, 1960; desk and chair by Alexandre Noll, ca. 1952.

Opposite
On the cabinet: *Important calice* ceramic by Georges Jouve, ca. 1955; pot by Mado Jolain, ca. 1960.
On the desk: ceramic by Valérie Hermans, 2012.

TEXAS

 Bowl by Takuro Kuwata, 2014.

Above
Hanging wall case by Paul Evans, Phillip Lloyd Powell, and George Nakashima, 1964.
On the shelves: box by Harrison McIntosh, ca. 1960; *Pomme bouche* artwork by Claude Lalanne, 1980.

Opposite
Elevational Weights, Vertical Mass artwork by Richard Serra, 2010; mobile by Jacques Jarrige, 2016; *PK55* table by Poul Kjaerholm, 1957; *Revolving Armchair No. 23* by Charlotte Perriand, 1949; *Metropole 305 Standard* chairs by Jean Prouvé, 1953.
On the table: jug by Valentine Schlegel, 1955; *Mousse Large Basin* ceramic by Jean Girel, 2011.

Following pages
Bo 961 chair by Jørgen Lund and Ole Larsen, 1961; *Slab* bench by George Nakashima, ca. 1960; *Minguren I* coffee table by George Nakashima, ca. 1955; *Elysée* sofa and armchair by Pierre Paulin, 1972-74; *Conoid* room divider by George Nakashima, 1984; *Contenir le vent "8-VI"* artwork by Brigitte Marionneau, 2019; *Untitled* artwork by Christopher Wool, 2016.
On the shelves: *Bouteilles épaulées, Roseaux* ceramics by Jacques and Dani Ruelland, 1970; artwork by Eva Hild, 2009.

Prince/Picasso
Jean Royère

Soft 2 ceramic by Helle Damkjaer, 2019; *Hibou* artwork by Paul Hanrez, 1995; *Important calice* ceramic by Georges Jouve, ca. 1955; box by Paul Evans, ca. 1970; ceramic bottles by Suzanne Ramié, 1952 and 1965; *Pansue*, *Figue*, *Boule Ovoïde*, and *Boule* ceramics by Jacques and Dani Ruelland, 1960.

Goutte d'eau table by Ado Chale, 1972; vases by Gustavo Pérez, 2005 and 2011; *Mousse Large Basin* ceramic by Jean Girel, 2011; *EKC22* chairs by Poul Kjaerholm, 1955.

CAB Foundation

Established in 2012 by the Belgian collector Hubert Bonnet, the CAB Foundation in Brussels is a non-profit space dedicated to the promotion of minimalist and conceptual art through a program of exhibitions and events. The Foundation is housed in a 750-square-meter 1933 Art Deco-style warehouse designed by A. Libotte[1] for the coal mining industry and renovated entirely by Olivier Dwek. It is set in the upscale Etangs d'Ixelles area near many other art venues. A flexible, modular design accommodates almost any kind of artistic experimentation. The Foundation, located at 32–34 Rue Borrens, also includes a studio for artists in residence. Citing his interest in Renzo Piano's Beyeler Foundation (Riehen, Switzerland, 1997) because of its use of natural light and "dematerialized space conducive to contemplation," Dwek made use of two skylights that run the entire length of the former warehouse. He conserved elements of the original building that continue to affirm its industrial origins at the same time as he installed the necessary systems for the conservation and exhibition of art. As in other examples of his work that willfully overlay an older structure with modern or contemporary elements, in the CAB Foundation he has not erased the 1933 building but has made it able to receive the most contemporary art in a coherent and attractive way.

1. See http://www.irismonument.be/fr.Ixelles.Rue_Borrens.html accessed March 28, 2020.

Following pages
Chairs by Jørgen Høj and Poul Kjaerholm, 1951;
Palazzo low table by Sébastien Caporusso;
stools by Stan Bitters, ca. 1960;
vase by Cécile Noguès, 2012.

Opposite
Diagonal Line artwork by Bernar Venet, 2020.

Previous pages
Diagonal Line artwork by Bernar Venet, 2020.
In the background: *Diagonal 68.5°* artwork by Bernar Venet, 1979.

Edouard Nortier Residence

This 460-square-meter triplex apartment in the chic Paris suburb of Neuilly-sur-Seine is located at the lower levels of a five-story 1980s building set on Rue Edouard Nortier. The architect was asked to unite the building's levels to create a coherent architectural and functional whole. The leitmotif in the décor is the use of shades of gray and black, first announced by the brushed-aluminum surfaces in the reception area. In fact, the gray tones were inspired by a specially created cast-aluminum *Goutte d'eau* dining table by Ado Chale measuring more than three meters. "We experimented with various gray-toned materials and with lines that echo the curved pattern of its top," says Dwek. The floors on the main level are finished with slabs of geometrically veined stone extracted from a riverbed. Full-height glazing allow the interiors to blend into the rear garden fully. In fact, there is a 27-meter view from the reception room through the living and dining space to the back of the garden. In the dining area, above the Ado Chale table, a 1958 three-branch ceiling light by Serge Mouille neighbors a large work by George Condo entitled *Diagonal Portrait* (2013). A large hanging glass piece by Jean-Michel Othoniel (*Collier Gris Mica*, 2018), continues the theme of black and gray. In the neighboring living space, a curving gray *Jelly Pea* sofa by India Mahdavi near a free-form coffee table by Ado Chale offers a note of comfort. Olivier Dwek personally designed many of the elements of the décor, including hand-brushed aluminum shelving and the matte-black master dressing room and bathroom with its double basin in natural honed stone. The basement level of the apartment makes space for a naturally lit 11-meter pool, a home cinema, and a spa with a hammam.

Opposite
Nuage bookcase by Charlotte Perriand, 1959; *Luge* deck chair by Jean Royère, ca. 1937; stools by Charlotte Perriand, ca. 1950–60; *Mad Cow* artwork by Christopher Wool, 1997.
On the bookshelf: ceramics by Pol Chambost and Jacques and Dani Ruelland.

Following pages
Jelly Pea sofa by India Mahdavi; *Arborescence* pedestal table by Eric Robin; coffee table by Ado Chale, 2012; *Minerale* artwork by Ritsue Mishima, 2004; carpet and curtains by Isabelle Reynders; *Committee* chairs by Pierre Jeanneret, ca. 1955; bench by Mira Nakashima, ca. 2000; *GH/M 446/1*, *Heller Quantensprung (John Mauss)* and *GH/M 446/2*, *Quantensprung (dunkel)* artworks by Gregor Hildebrandt, 2011.
On the shelves: *Chaotic* artwork by Klara Kristalova, 2012; *Composition* ceramic by Louisélio, 2010; *Unknown poet #6* artwork by Hernan Bas, 2012.

DRINK
Coca-Cola
Z3

Opposite
Untitled (Z3) artwork by Jannis Kounellis, 1961; *Smoker Study #7* artwork by Tom Wesselmann, 1967; *Untitled (Coca Cola)* artwork by Jean-Michel Basquiat, 1982; (right) *EXHM/DS3* artwork by Sterling Ruby, 2011; *Or* floor lamp by Eric Robin; stools by Charlotte Perriand, ca. 1950–60.

Above
Coque wall light by Hervé Van der Straeten, 2004; *Collier Gris Mica* by Jean-Michel Othoniel, 2018; chair by Alexandre Noll, ca. 1940.

Above
Not There (left and right) artwork by Louise Lawler, 2003–04; wall cabinet by George Nakashima, ca. 1969; *Ice Cream Ball* ceramics by Tony Marsh, 2012.

Opposite
GH/M 446/1, Heller Quantensprung (John Mauss) and *GH/M 446/2, Quantensprung (dunkel)* artworks by Gregor Hildebrandt, 2011; chair by Alexandre Noll, ca. 1940; ceramics by Kristin McKirdy, 2019.

Previous pages
Goutte d'eau dining table by Ado Chale, 2010; *Metropole 306 Standard* chairs by Jean Prouvé, 1952; *Office* chair by Pierre Jeanneret, ca. 1955; *Untitled* artwork by Paola Pivi, 2016; ceiling light by Serge Mouille, 1958; *Diagonal Portrait* artwork by George Condo, 2013.
On the table: ceramics by Tony Marsh, 2010; *Leaf* plate by Peter Lane.

Opposite
Bowl by John Pawson; kitchen designed by Obumex, 2009. Bead-blasted stainless steel, etched gray-glass extractor hood in a metal frame, dark sucupira, honed natural stone.
On the wall: *Eye #4 (Roadside Victim)* artwork by Alex Prager, 2012.

Above
Bespoke double basin in natural honed stone by Olivier Dwek, 2009.

Opposite
A331 Beehive ceiling lamp by Alvar Aalto, 1953; *Où et Quand? Nulle Part. Question 6* artwork by Sophie Calle, 2012; ceramics by Jacques and Dani Ruelland, ca. 1970.

Sophie Calle Prenez soin de vous
Cindy Sherman

Following pages
Left: *Goutte d'eau* dining table by Ado Chale, 2010; ceramics by Tony Marsh, 2010.
Right: *Neutra* armchairs by Vincent Van Duysen, 2008; natural stone floor, 2009.

Silver House

Zante, or Zakynthos in Greek, is one of the largest of the Ionian Islands. The Silver House was built at a high point of relatively untouched land at the north of the island, facing Cephalonia, which lies 15 kilometers further north. The architect explains that the design is a 21st-century reinterpretation of the vernacular architecture of the Greek islands. The entirely white house faced by a three-sided infinity pool almost literally draws in the blues of the sky and the Ionian Sea. Sensitive to contemporary art, Olivier Dwek references the work of the French artist Yves Klein (1928–62), who said: "Blue has no dimensions, it is beyond dimensions." Here the vast expanses of sea and sky certainly confirm that idea. The forms and openings of the house seek both to frame views and to protect residents from the sun and wind. One goal is certainly to remove any possible barriers between interiors and the outdoors and to provide panoramic views from every area of the house. To these ends, sliding glass walls open entirely and the same cladding materials, such as the locally sourced white stone floors, are used both for the exterior and the interior. Olivier Dwek refers to a composition made up of glass boxes and patios, of voids and solids. The essentially rectangular plan includes four bedrooms, with the master bedroom suite as the only volume on the upper level. The dining area is in the central patio between the kitchen and living spaces. The sophisticated geometric composition seen in elevations might bring to mind Cubist or De Stijl designs, and is willfully contrasted with the rough, stony environment.

Natural stone floor and polished concrete terraces and an infinity pool with three vanishing edges looking out to the southern point of Cephalonia.

Natural black stone kitchen work surface and black thermo-painted aluminium corner sliding doors.

Previous pages
Relief lunaire dining table by Ado Chale, 2012; *Heritage* stacking chairs by Philippe Starck, 2001; *Arceau* artwork by Ado Chale, ca. 2009; bowl by Ado Chale, ca. 2012.

Opposite
Barcelona daybed and coffee table by Ludwig Mies van der Rohe, 1929; folding easy chairs by Johan Hagen, 1958; *Harlem Paper* artwork by Jean-Michel Basquiat, 1987.

Following pages
View from the bathroom of the master bedroom to Cephalonia, through two windows that surround the staircase.

EAR WAX
EQUATOR
GLASS EYE
TESLACOIL
HORIZON
EQUATOR
HORIZON
TESLA COIL
EAR WAX

Etangs d'Ixelles Town House

The area of Etangs d'Ixelles, located near two long narrow ponds, is considered one of the most attractive parts of the European capital. Olivier Dwek was called in to renovate a 370-square-meter, five-story 1930s town house on Rue Vilain XIIII that runs perpendicular to the ponds. The client was a young businessman and art collector with a taste for ceramics and Modernist furniture. The ground floor of the house has an entrance hall and a dining room including a discrete kitchen. The architect singled out the volumes and light in the dining room, heightened by a large *Bleach Collage* by the American artist Sterling Ruby, a plywood *Plug* table by the fashion designer Rick Owens with chairs by Pierre Jeanneret and Jean Prouvé, and a powerful contemporary ceramic work by Akiyama Yo. A double living room is located on the next level up. Here, a *Joséphine* table in bronze by Ado Chale, a *PK80* daybed by Poul Kjaerholm, and *Committee* chairs by Pierre Jeanneret neighbor artwork by Thomas Houseago and a large colored woodcut by the Romanian brothers Gert and Uwe Tobias. The house has a total of four bedrooms located on the two upper levels, including the master bedroom suite. The street façade of the house was restored, as were the original doors and windows. Olivier Dwek designed the new back façade as well as the interior volumes. In collaboration with the owner, the architect selected pieces of historic modern furniture by Pierre Jeanneret and Jean Prouvé. One signature piece in the house is a chest *(bahut)* designed by Le Corbusier for the Cité Radieuse (Marseille, 1952). Olivier Dwek says that the architecture and the interior volumes were in fact thought out to exhibit artworks, and to encourage a dialogue between architecture, design, and art.

Opposite
Ceiling light by Serge Mouille, 1958; *Antony* shelving unit by Jean Prouvé, ca. 1953; ceramics by Jacques and Dani Ruelland and Suzanne Ramié, ca. 1950 and 1970; *Pyramids and Worlds* artwork by Alexander Calder, 1970; *Nothing but Flowers* artwork by Thomas Lerooy, 2011.

Following pages
150BC sofa by Vladimir Kagan, ca. 1950; *Kangourou* fireside chair by Pierre Jeanneret, ca. 1955; stools by Charlotte Perriand, ca. 1950–60; *Joséphine* coffee table by Ado Chale, 2013; *PK80* daybed by Poul Kjaerholm, ca. 1950; *Committee* chairs by Pierre Jeanneret, ca. 1955; *Bench from Cité Cansado* by Charlotte Perriand, ca. 1958; *Untitled* artwork by Gert and Uwe Tobias, 2005; *Infinito* artwork by Ritsue Mishima, 2015; *Flesh of the Shadow Spirits 60* artwork by Kendell Geers, 2011.
On the table: ceramic by Takuro Kuwata, 2015.

Olivier Dwek
THE IMPOSSIBLE COLLECTION OF DESIGN

Opposite
Untitled artwork by Thomas Houseago, 2015; *Committee* chair by Pierre Jeanneret, ca. 1955; *PK80* daybed by Poul Kjaerholm, ca. 1950; *Joséphine* coffee table by Ado Chale, 2013.

Following pages
Base-building pigeonhole desk by Pierre Jeanneret, ca. 1957; *Office* chair by Pierre Jeanneret, ca. 1955.

GILBERT & GEORGE

DIT/CT-58
VOL 1 GILBERT & GEORGE TATE
VOL 2 GILBERT & GEORGE TATE
ASSOULINE
PHILLIPS

Expansion Bock artwork by César, 1970; *Louis XXI, porcelaine humaine* artwork by Andrea Branzi, 2010; *Pink Clown* from *PROPO* series by Paul McCarthy, 1991.

Opposite
BC (4384) artwork by Sterling Ruby, 2013; *Plug* table by Rick Owens; *Type* chairs by Pierre Jeanneret, ca. 1955; *Metropole 306 Standard* chairs by Jean Prouvé, 1952.
On the table: ceramic by Akiyama Yo, 2014.

Following pages
Bench by Pierre Jeanneret, ca. 1955.

N.E.S.T. Foundation

N.E.S.T. is a privileged location for the exhibition of contemporary art created by Olivier Dwek for a major Belgian collector. It is intended as a cultural meeting place for start-ups, a kind of incubator. The industrial building, set in the countryside between Ghent and Kortrijk where N.E.S.T. is located, offers an area of 1,250 square meters on the ground floor and a further 750 square meters on the upper level. The collector, who is a patron of the Museum Dhondt-Dhaenens (Deurle, Belgium), is interested not only in contemporary art, but also in modern furniture, in vintage automobiles (exhibited in the southern portion of the ground floor), and in music. The client requested that acoustics be of the highest quality to allow for concerts organized by the Queen Elisabeth Music Chapel. Olivier Dwek conceived a system that allows fins that regulate natural lighting to also serve as elements in the acoustic design. The ground-floor exhibition rooms offer ceiling heights of seven to eight meters. Dwek's idea was to give an impression of monolithic walls and floors, forming a kind of case to privilege the art. A light-gray cement finish on the walls was carefully matched with a liquid cement screed. Central walls were finished in white at the request of the client. A meeting room and library are located on a mezzanine level. In this space a hand-hammered tin bar designed by Olivier Dwek sits beneath three hanging lamps by the noted Belgian designer Jules Wabbes (1919–74).

Untitled artwork by Danh Vo, 2016;
We the People (detail) artwork by Danh Vo, 2011–16; *Paper Drop (passage) VI* artwork by Wolfgang Tillmans, 2019.

Corona
Victoria

We the People (detail) artworks by Danh Vo, 2011–16; *No-Rat Box* artworks by Danh Vo, 2010.

Corona
Victoria

Untitled (F52) artwork by Christopher Wool, 1992; *Refuse* artwork by Gavin Turk, 2012; *And I Trust You* artwork by Tracey Emin, 2015.

And I Trust You
ANDIFYOU
CANTTAKE
AJOKEYOU
CANGETTHE
FUCKOUTOF
MYHOUSE

PARTIAL
TRVTH.

Opposite
Anthropomorphe floor lamp by Philippe Hiquily, 1993; *Untitled ("Club" Fauteuil)* armchair by Franz West, 2015; *Cloud* coffee table by Jacques Hervouet; ceramics by Kristin McKirdy, 2018; *Poisson* dish by Séraphin Soudbinine; *Waiting for Godot* ceramics by Sejin Bae, 2019; *On the Rocks* sofa by Francesco Binfare, 2004; *Silence is Golden/ Talk or Die* artwork by Bruce Nauman, 1983; *Geiler Gaul* artwork by Franz West, 2005; *Bagatelle* artwork by Franz West, 1982; *Partial Truth* artwork by Bruce Nauman, 1997.

Above
Untitled artwork by Günther Förg, 2007.

Previous pages
Divan by Franz West, 1998; *Untitled ("Club" Fauteuil)* armchair by Franz West, 2015; *Untitled* artwork by Christopher Wool, 1998; *Studies for Holograms (a-e)* artworks by Bruce Nauman, 1970.

Opposite
S.A.M TS 11 table by Jean Prouvé, ca. 1942; *Tout bois* chairs by Jean Prouvé, 1953; *Large Swan, Small Shell* and *Large Flower* vases by Malene Knudsen, 2020; *Codex Monotypes #30* artwork by Julie Mehretu, 2018; *Painting for T.* artwork by Secundino Hernández, 2017.

Above
Nature's Privy Seal artwork by Jason Rhoades, 2003.

Above
Bar by Olivier Dwek, 2019; *MT 344* stool by Pierre Chareau, 1926; pendant by Jules Wabbes, nickel-plated brass, 1968.

Opposite
Table by Arne Jacobsen, 1956–58; *PK9* chairs by Poul Kjaerholm, ca. 1961; *Totem* candleholders by Franck Evennou; *Large Blue Starfish* vase by Antoinette Faragallah; golden cups by Shizue Imai; candleholders by Pierre Forssel, between 1967 and 1978.

Arbeitstisch in Aspik table by Franz West, 2008; *Tout bois* chair by Jean Prouvé, 1953; *Boule*, *Bilobé*, *Ovoïde*, and *Balustre* vases by Louis Lourioux; *The Drawers and I* desk by Martin Szekely, 2018; *Soft Pad* chair by Charles and Ray Eames, ca. 1950; table lamp by George Nakashima, 1973; boxes by Alexandre Noll, ca. 1950; trilobe vase and two-handle vase by Henri Simmen.

Le Corbusier Meubles et intérieurs 1905-1965

Ox chairs by Hans Wegner, 1960; *Aztèque* coffee tables by Agnès Debizet, 2020; *1089* vase by Pol Chambost, 1955; *Pansu* vase by Georges Jouve, 1956; *Boule aplatie* vase by Georges Jouve, 1957; *Patte d'ours* ashtray by Georges Jouve, 1951.

Low table by André Aleth Masson, 1962; *Camaleonda* modular sofa by Mario Bellini, 1970; *Nénuphar* floor lamp by Philippe Hiquily, 1985; *The Algiers' Sections of a Happy Moment* artwork by David Claerbout, 2010; *Matterhorn* artwork by Kris Martin, 2009; *Trompette* floor lamp by Pierre Paulin, ca. 1970.
On the screen: *Metropolis,* film by Fritz Lang, 1927.

Les Mélèzes Town House

The starting point for this project is an exceptional three-story town house in Brussels, designed in the Beaux-Arts style by François Kielbaey in 1912 with a garage and apartment annex added in 1927 by the architect J. L'Ancre.[1] The house is remarkable in Brussels not only because of its size and quality but also because it has three façades as opposed to the more frequent local configuration of two visible elevations. The topmost level is lodged beneath a mansard roof. Olivier Dwek's spectacular renovation of this elegant house, with its restored French limestone façades, retained the original form of the curved windows, fireplaces, and moldings. All the woodwork on the walls and the moldings in the living room and reception areas were fully restored. A central staircase with a wrought-iron balustrade was extended upward in the same style toward a skylight. As is frequently the case in the work of Olivier Dwek, opening the structure and bringing in more light is an important element in this design. Rather than a more classical, relatively closed town house, he has generated a bright, open volume. Here, as in other projects, Olivier Dwek has contrasted both his own architectural intervention and the original house with modern furniture designed by Charlotte Perriand, Pierre Jeanneret, and others. Similarly, the works in the house by the English and American contemporary artists Thomas Houseago, Jacob Kassay, and Christopher Wool were "curated around the theme of silver." According to Dwek, this willful contrast and juxtapositions of periods is "superposed in three layers that communicate like a palimpsest."

1. See http://www.irismonument.be/fr.Ixelles.Rue_Borrens.html accessed March 28, 2020.

Following pages
Left: *Poire* ceramic by Georges Jouve, ca. 1955.
Right: *High Court Down* sofa by Pierre Jeanneret, ca. 1955; *Slab* coffee table by George Nakashima, 1963; daybed by Charlotte Perriand, ca. 1956–59; *Untitled* artwork by Jacob Kassay, 2012.
On the table: *Poire* ceramic by Georges Jouve, ca. 1955; ceramic by Georges Jouve, ca. 1945.

Opposite
Reclining Figure artwork by Thomas Houseago, 2008; *Office* chair by Pierre Jeanneret, ca. 1955.

Jean Royère

Above and opposite
Untitled (Placebo) installation by Simon Nicaise, 2010; *Ombre* chair by Charlotte Perriand, 1958.

Following pages
Bridge Director armchair by Jean Prouvé, ca. 1950; desk by Pierre Jeanneret, ca. 1955; *SP230* artwork by Sterling Ruby, 2013.

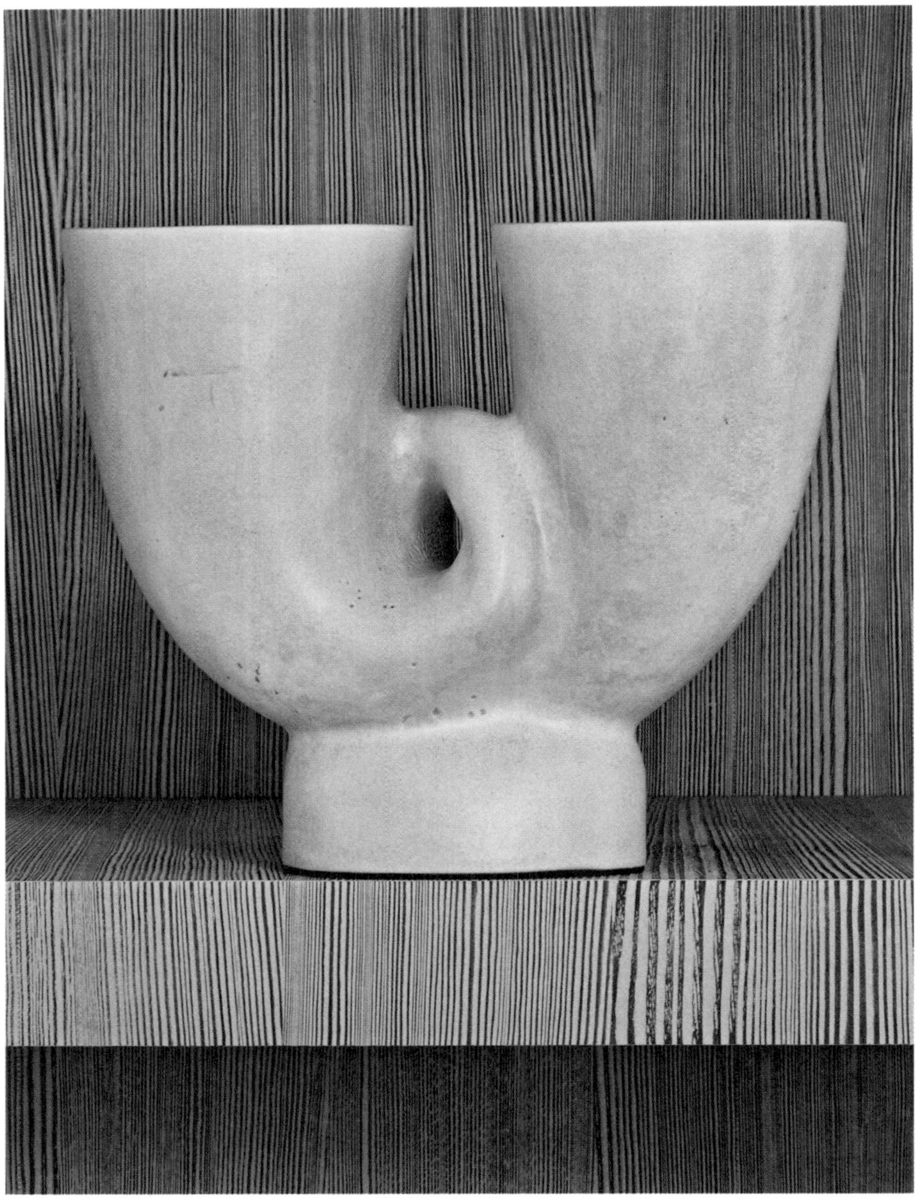

Above
Ceramic by Georges Jouve, ca. 1945.

Opposite
Bookcase by Olivier Dwek, 2008.
In the bookcase: Dogon Walu mask, Mali; Keaka statue, Cameroon or Nigeria; "white" mask, Fang or Okande, Gabon; *Transcompositional/Fur + Tattoo* artwork by Sterling Ruby, 2009.

LAMPSHADES
WOOL

Table by Charlotte Perriand, 1949; *Untitled (P 583)* artwork by Christopher Wool, 2009; stools by Charlotte Perriand, ca. 1950–60.

Above
Afterimage 09-330 artwork
by Byung Hoon Choï, 2009.

Opposite
The French limestone façade designed
by the architect François Kielbaey in 1912,
restored by Olivier Dwek in 2008.

10

Seaflower Residence

Knokke-le-Zoute is a fashionable North Sea beach resort located a few kilometers from the border between Belgium and the Netherlands. The intervention of Olivier Dwek concerns a fourth- and fifth-floor, 360-square-meter, duplex penthouse facing the sea in a modern building designed by the Belgian architect Marc Corbiau (1980). The main (fourth) floor, which includes two bedrooms, has an area of 230 square meters with an additional 62 square meters of terraces. The smaller fifth floor has 100 square meters of indoor area and 115 square meters of terraces with a view on the sea. Olivier Dwek states that in this instance he worked more as a curator for the collections of art and furniture, and a scenographer for their placement, than he did as an architect. Some elements of the apartment design, such as wall placements, were updated, and he specifically designed a free-form rug for the living space. Works by Jean-Michel Basquiat, Donald Judd, Bruce Nauman, and Andy Warhol neighbor furniture by George Nakashima, Alexandre Noll, or Jean Royère. Also part of the collection are a number of African works, including Kota reliquaries (Gabon) and a Baoulé statue from the Cote d'Ivoire, that are displayed in the library designed by Axel Vervoordt. A living room group of furniture by Jean Prouvé (from the collection of Claude Berri) and Charlotte Perriand is placed near a terrace and an open dining area. The upper-floor suite includes a floor piece by Carl Andre and works by Wolfgang Laib, Günther Förg, Rudolf Stingel, Christopher Wool, and Sol LeWitt.

It Doesn't Matter My Friend, It Does Not Matter, To Cry Is Beautiful artwork by Tracey Emin, 2004; *Ninth Copper Cardinal* artwork by Carl Andre, 1973; *Stag* stool by Rick Owens, 2015.

It doesn't matter
My Friend it does
Not matter
To Cry is Beautiful

Opposite
Chair by Alexandre Noll, ca. 1940; *Library* chairs by Pierre Jeanneret, ca. 1960; *East Indian Laurel Frenchmans Cove* table by George Nakashima. *Hekiyu Renmonki* ceramic by Yoshiro Kimura, 2015.

Above
Double Large Figures artwork by Juan Muñoz, 1991; *Untitled* artwork by Secundino Hernández, 2016.

Above
En Peau armchair by Charlotte Perriand, 1946; *Untitled* artwork by Jean-Michel Basquiat, 1981; *Flaque* coffee table by Jean Royère, ca. 1952; two openings vase and *Cratère* vase by Georges Jouve, 1950 and 1957.

Opposite
Untitled "stack" artwork by Donald Judd, 1965; *Tokyo* bench by Charlotte Perriand, ca. 1950.
On the bench: Ceramic by Kristin McKirdy, 2016.

BASQUIAT
JEAN PROUVÉ
JEAN PROUVÉ
JEAN PROUVÉ

Previous pages
Ours polaire sofa and armchair by Jean Royère, ca. 1950; stool by Charlotte Perriand, ca. 1950–60; *Warthog* floor lamp by Richard Texier, 2019; *En Peau* armchair by Charlotte Perriand, 1946; *Flaque* coffee table by Jean Royère, ca. 1952; two openings vase and *Cratère* vase by Georges Jouve, 1950 and 1957; chairs by Alexandre Noll, ca. 1940; *Library* chair by Pierre Jeanneret, ca. 1960; *East Indian Laurel Frenchmans Cove* table by George Nakashima; *Hekiyu Renmonki* ceramic by Yoshiro Kimura, 2015; *La Liberté de l'esprit* artwork by René Magritte, 1949; *Cavalier et cheval* pitcher by Pablo Picasso, 1952; *Péril extra jaune* artwork by James Ensor, 1938; Lega mask, Congo Basin, early 20th century.

Opposite
Carpet by Olivier Dwek, 2016; stools by Charlotte Perriand, ca. 1950–60; *Forme libre* table by Charlotte Perriand, 1967; *Bridge Director* armchair by Jean Prouvé, ca. 1950; *Tea bowl* ceramic by Takuro Kuwata, 2016; *Cadeau* artwork by Man Ray, 1921–70; *Quintet* artwork by Berend Strik, 2002; *Untitled* artwork by Dan Van Severen, 1979; *Untitled* artwork by Wolfgang Laib, 2001; *Leaping Hare (facing right)* artwork by Barry Flanagan, 1996; *De Gendarmen* artwork by James Ensor, 1888; *Fourmi* and *Petite Voile* ceramics by Georges Jouve, ca. 1950 and 1957; *Swing-Jib* lamp by Jean Prouvé, 1957; *Figue* vase by Georges Jouve, ca. 1950; *Banana* bowl by Georges Jouve, ca. 1955; *Untitled* photograph by Ludwig Vandevelde, 1987; *Monument for the Romantic Poet (Oscar Wilde)* artwork by Barry Flanagan, 1990; *We the People (detail)* by Danh Vo, 2011–16; Dan masks, Ivory Coast; Kota reliquary statues, Gabon, late 19th century–early 20th century.

JAZZ
JEAN PROUVE
WORDS AND COINS
Manzoni

 Lapis artwork by Terry Winters, 2014.

Above
MAR.11,1990, painting by On Kawara, 1990; *Bagatelle* artwork by Franz West, 1982.

Opposite
Zen Print #1 and *Zen Print #2* artworks by Brice Marden, 2010; *B* candlestick by Richard Texier, 2009; *Cornet* vase and *Coq* pitcher vase by Roger Capron, 1955 and 1956; high stools by Pierre Jeanneret, ca. 1965.

Opposite
Jackie artwork by Andy Warhol, 1964.

Following pages
Imagine artwork by Tracey Emin, 2007; *Yes* artwork by Tracey Emin, 2007; *The Prophet* artwork by Francis Alÿs, 2001; *No Title (The Place, The...)* artwork by Raymond Pettibon, 1992; *No Title (What Was Before)* artwork by Raymond Pettibon, 2002; *Untitled (WMD, no. 4D)* artwork by Robert Longo, 2007; *The Angel* artwork by Michaël Borremans, 2014; *Coming on the Floor* artwork by Tracey Emin, 2007; *Never Again* artwork by Tracey Emin, 2007; *No Title (To the Owner...)* artwork by Raymond Pettibon, 2003; *Untitled* artworks by Francis Alÿs, 2004; *Deux couleurs* artwork by Willem Cole, 2006; *Nicht Hier 1* artwork by Wolfgang Laib, 1996; *Map no. 39* artwork by Tom Molloy, 2006; *Mocho* stool by Sergio Rodrigues, ca. 1960; floor lamp by Richard Texier, 2019.

SO SORRY FORGIVE ME PLEASE

Above
Double Poke in the Eye II artwork by Bruce Nauman, 1985.

Opposite
Untitled artwork by Rudolf Stingel, 1989; *1 2 3 4 5 4 3 2 1* artwork by Sol LeWitt, 1987.

Tout bois chair by Jean Prouvé, 1953;
S.A.M TS 11 table, Jean Prouvé, ca. 1942;
Waterways artwork by Ritsue Mishima, 2017;
Amor Fati Leaning artwork by Sterling Ruby, 2017; *Untitled* artwork by Günther Förg, 1989;
Weed artwork by Tony Matelli, 2007;
Stag stool by Rick Owens, 2015.

HANS OP DE BEECK
A passion for Jean Prouvé

Sofa by René Drouet, ca. 1950; floor lamp by Georges Jouve, ca. 1955; *DC1902* coffee table by Vincenzo De Cotiis, 2019; *Kangourou* fireside chair by Pierre Jeanneret, ca. 1955; stools by Charlotte Perriand, ca. 1950–60; *Reishaus* artwork by Wolfgang Laib, 2002. **On the table:** Nkondi Kongo-Vili Fetiche statue, Congo Basin, early 20th century; ceramics by Takuro Kuwata, 2014 and 2018.

Acknowledgments

To Louis Vuitton, for the trust they placed in me when I was very young.

To Ado Chale, a superb 20th-century decorative artist,
who trained my eye in beauty during my early youth.

To Philip Jodidio, one of the most widely read authors on architecture,
who fell in love with our creations and set off this magical adventure.

To Harry and Théodora, who light up each day of my life.

To our amazing patrons who grant us deep, artistic trust,
which in turn make many wonderful projects happen.

To my father, who inspired me to see things through.

To my mother, who nurtured my deep self-esteem.

To Catherine Bonifassi for her coordination of this book
and for her expertise.

To Thibaut Mathieu, Sarah de Beaumont, and their teams
for their eagle eyes.

To the mother of my children for her insight and artistic direction
on the Seaflower residence and the photoshoots in Greece.

To Catherine and Marc for their unconditional support in my quest
for art over many years.

To the architects, partners, and collaborators from past and present:
Pierre Haccour, Aristide Van Roy, Gil Dupuis, Carl-Eric de Sivers,
Nicolas De Bruyn, Mathieu Dewitte, Thuy Vo, Marjolijn Bijman,
Julie Ruquois, Laura Olivieri, Jonathan Israel, Valentin Bosquart,
Grégory Eyndels, Noémie Schrager, Benoit Hoyas, Jean-Marc Rosillon,
Émilie Yannoudis, Fabienne Nogaret, Céline Vanderstraeten,
and to all those who made a difference in the history of the agency.

To all the craftspeople, with their extraordinary savoir faire,
without whom our projects wouldn't have soul and magic.

To all our photographers, Philippe, Jarmo, Jérôme,
Serge, Belén, and Jean-François.

Credits

Cover

Untitled sculpture – (Gong), Bally, PA artwork by Harry Bertoia, ca. 1960, steel © SABAM Belgium, 2021; *Two Guys Twice* artwork by Richard Prince, 2001-02, acrylic on canvas, Charles Riva collection © Richard Prince; *Alta* lounge chair by Oscar Niemeyer, 1972, steel, wool and plywood © NIEMEYER, OSCAR / SABAM Belgium, 2021; *Ours polaire* armchair and sofa by Jean Royère, 1947, wood, and fabric © SABAM Belgium, 2021; *Flaque* coffee table by Jean Royère, 1960, wood, formica and zinc © SABAM Belgium, 2021; carpet by Maurice Pré, 1947, wool © SABAM Belgium, 2021; *Chardons* chandelier by Hubert Le Gall, 2018, bronze © SABAM Belgium, 2021.

Introduction

Page 12
Velin chairs by Christian Liaigre, 1998, wood and leather; dining table by Ado Chale, 2007, resin and mosaic of bone quills, courtesy Studio Ado Chale © SABAM Belgium, 2021; bookcase by Obumex, 2006, oak and alpaca, Olivier Dwek collection; wall sconces by Jules Wabbes, ca. 1960, anodized aluminum; *Grand Bassin* by Jean Girel, 2011, porcelain © SABAM Belgium, 2021.

Pages 18-19
Neutra armchair by Vincent Van Duysen, 2008, aluminum; ceramic by Takayuki Sakiyama, 2015, courtesy Pierre Marie Giraud, Brussels; stools by Charlotte Perriand, ca. 1950–60, oak, courtesy Laffanour Galerie Downtown © SABAM Belgium, 2021.

Page 22
White Snow Dwarf (Dopey #2) artwork by Paul McCarthy, 2012, silicone, Olivier Dwek collection, courtesy the Artist and Xavier Hufkens, Brussels; *Mother & Son* artwork by Louise Bourgeois, 2007, gouache on paper, Olivier Dwek collection, courtesy Hauser & Wirth © Louise Bourgeois Trust / SABAM Belgium, 2021; ceramics by Kristin McKirdy, 2015, Olivier Dwek collection, courtesy Pierre Marie Giraud, Brussels; *Pink and White Cloud* and *Turquoise and White Cloud* ceramics by Bente Skjøttgaard, 2014, Olivier Dwek collection © Bente Skjøttgaard – Galerie Pierre Marie Giraud – Galerie Maria Lund; *5005* coffee table by Paul Frankl, ca. 1948, Olivier Dwek collection; sideboard by Jean Prouvé, ca. 1950, steel sheet and wood, Olivier Dwek collection, courtesy Laffanour Galerie Downton © SABAM Belgium, 2021; *Visiteur* armchair by Jean Prouvé, ca. 1948, oak, sheet steel, and fabric, Olivier Dwek collection, courtesy Laffanour Galerie Downton © SABAM Belgium, 2021; *Standard* chair by Jean Prouvé, ca. 1950, sheet steel and cast plywood, Olivier Dwek collection, courtesy Laffanour Galerie Downton © SABAM Belgium, 2021; *Swing Jib* lamp by Jean Prouvé, ca. 1947, metal and steel, cable, Olivier Dwek collection, courtesy Laffanour Galerie Downton © SABAM Belgium, 2021.

Australian House

Pages 28-29
Cube chairs by Gunnar Aagaard Andersen, 1980, leather stripes, courtesy New Hope Gallery © SABAM Belgium, 2021; *EKC24* lounge chair by Poul Kjaerholm, 1965, stainless steel, cane, and leather, courtesy New Hope Gallery; *EKC62* side table by Poul Kjaerholm, 1968, stainless steel, Forsgrunn marble, courtesy New Hope Gallery; *S.C.A.L.* daybed by Jean Prouvé, 1954, steel, and upholstery, courtesy Laffanour Galerie Downtown © SABAM Belgium, 2021.

Page 36
Son of Bozo artwork by George Condo, 2009, oil on linen, Olivier Dwek collection, courtesy Galerie Xavier Hufkens © SABAM Belgium, 2021; ceramics by Tony Marsh, 2015, courtesy Pierre Marie Giraud, Brussels; ceramic by Yoshiro Kimura, 2015, courtesy Pierre Marie Giraud, Brussels; stools by Charlotte Perriand, ca. 1950–60, oak, courtesy Laffanour Galerie Downtown © SABAM Belgium, 2021; *Clam* chair by Philip Arctander, ca. 1940, sheepskin and beech, courtesy New Hope Gallery; *Grass-Seated* chairs by George Nakashima, ca. 1950, seagrass and walnut, courtesy New Hope Gallery; *PH5/3* floor lamp by Poul Henningsen, ca. 1930, metal, brass, and copper, courtesy New Hope Gallery; *Conoid* dining table by George Nakashima, 1971, American black walnut, courtesy New Hope Gallery.

Page 37
Ceramics by Tony Marsh, 2015, courtesy Pierre Marie Giraud, Brussels; ceramic by Yoshiro Kimura, 2015, courtesy Pierre Marie Giraud, Brussels; *Conoid* dining table by George Nakashima, 1971, American black walnut, courtesy New Hope Gallery.

Pages 38-39
Banana sofa by Otto Schultz, ca. 1950, wool and wood, courtesy New Hope Gallery; *Goutte d'eau* table by Ado Chale, ca. 1970, bronze, courtesy New Hope Gallery © SABAM Belgium, 2021; artwork by Ib Geertsen, 1950, bronze, courtesy New Hope Gallery and Galleri Tom Christoffersen; *White Cloud* ceramic by Bente Skjøttgaard, 2017, Olivier Dwek collection © Bente Skjøttgaard – Galerie Pierre Marie Giraud – Galerie Maria Lund; *PK80* daybed by Poul Kjaerholm, ca. 1950, steel and leather, Olivier Dwek collection; *Minguren II* side table by George Nakashima, ca. 1965, oak burl, courtesy New Hope Gallery; stools by Charlotte Perriand, ca. 1950–1960, oak, courtesy Laffanour Galerie Downtown © SABAM Belgium, 2021.

Pages 40-41
Forme libre table by Charlotte Perriand, ca. 1960, ash, courtesy Laffanour Galerie Downtown © SABAM Belgium, 2021; *Bridge Director* armchair by Jean Prouvé, ca. 1950, leather, oak, and lacquered steel, courtesy Laffanour Galerie Downtown © SABAM Belgium, 2021; *PH4/3* table lamps by Poul Henningsen, ca. 1930, metal, brass, and copper, courtesy New Hope Gallery.

Pages 42-43
Table Bench by Finn Juhl, ca. 1955, steel, brass, and wood, courtesy New Hope Gallery; *Spin* artwork by Ritsue Mishima, 2017, glass, courtesy Pierre Marie Giraud, Brussels; *S.C.A.L.* daybed by Jean Prouvé, 1954, steel and upholstery, courtesy Laffanour Galerie Downtown © SABAM Belgium, 2021.

Pages 46-47
S.C.A.L. daybed by Jean Prouvé, 1954, steel and upholstery, courtesy Laffanour Galerie Downtown © SABAM Belgium, 2021.

New Hope Collection

Page 51
Untitled sculpture – (Gong), Bally, PA artwork by Harry Bertoia, ca. 1960, steel © SABAM Belgium, 2021; *Two Guys Twice* artwork by Richard Prince, 2001-02, acrylic on canvas, Charles Riva collection © Richard Prince; *Alta* lounge chair by Oscar Niemeyer, 1972, steel, wool, and plywood © NIEMEYER, OSCAR / SABAM Belgium, 2021; *Ours polaire* armchair and sofa by Jean Royère, 1947, wood and fabric © SABAM Belgium, 2021; *Flaque* coffee table by Jean Royère, 1960, wood, formica, and zinc © SABAM Belgium, 2021; carpet by Maurice Pré, 1947, wool © SABAM Belgium, 2021; *Chardons* candlestick by Hubert Le Gall, 2018, bronze © SABAM Belgium, 2021.

Page 52
Hanging wall cabinet by George Nakashima, ca. 1965, American walnut and wicker, courtesy New Hope Gallery; ceramic bottles by Suzanne Ramié, atelier Madoura, 1952 and 1965, courtesy Thomas Fritsch – Artrium; *Pansue, Figue, Boule Ovoïde,* and *Boule* ceramics by Jacques and Dani Ruelland, 1960, courtesy Thomas Fritsch – Artrium © SABAM Belgium, 2021.

Page 53
Lightning vase by Marc du Plantier, 1940, plaster, courtesy Galerie Anne-Sophie Duval; ceramics by Valérie Hermans, 2012, courtesy the artist and Galerie Arcanes; *Alta* lounge chair by Oscar Niemeyer, 1972, steel, wool, and plywood, Daniel Lebard collection © NIEMEYER, OSCAR / SABAM Belgium, 2021; *Ours polaire* armchair by Jean Royère, 1947, wood and fabric © SABAM Belgium, 2021; *Flaque* coffee table by Jean Royère, 1960, wood, formica, and zinc © SABAM Belgium, 2021; carpet by Maurice Pré, 1947, wool © SABAM Belgium, 2021; *Chardons* candlestick by Hubert Le Gall, 2018, bronze © SABAM Belgium, 2021.

Pages 54-55
Boomerang desk by Jules Wabbes, 1957, mutényé and steel, Laurent Gutmer collection, courtesy New Hope Gallery; *Babel* ceramic by Turi Heisselberg Pedersen, 2019, stoneware, courtesy Mouvements Modernes Gallery; *MR 10* chairs by Ludwig Mies van der Rohe, 1927, steel and rattan, Daniel Lebard collection © SABAM Belgium, 2021; box by Paul Evans, ca. 1970, resin and bronze, courtesy New Hope Gallery; ceramic by Georges Jouve, 1955, ceramic, metal, and nylon, courtesy Thomas Fritsch – Artrium; hanging wall shelf by George Nakashima, ca. 1960, American black walnut, courtesy New Hope Gallery; ceramic by André Borderie, ca. 1960, courtesy Thomas Fritsch – Artrium; *Lamp* painting by Philip Guston, 1979, oil on canvas, Charles Riva collection © The Estate of Philip Guston; *Alta* lounge chair by Oscar Niemeyer, 1972, steel, wool, and plywood © NIEMEYER, OSCAR / SABAM Belgium, 2021; *Ours polaire* armchair and sofa by Jean Royère, 1947, wood and fabric © SABAM Belgium, 2021; *Flaque coffee* table by Jean Royère, 1960, wood, formica, and zinc © SABAM Belgium, 2021.

Page 57
Alta lounge chair armchair by Oscar Niemeyer, 1972, steel, wool, and plywood © NIEMEYER, OSCAR / SABAM Belgium, 2021; *Ours polaire* armchair and sofa by Jean Royère, 1947, wood and fabric © SABAM Belgium, 2021; *Flaque* coffee table by Jean Royère, 1960, wood, formica, and zinc © SABAM Belgium, 2021; wall sconce by Jules Wabbes, 1969, bronze; *Zombie* armchair by Roger Tallon, 1967, polyester, fiberglass, vinyl, and steel.

Page 58
Cabinet by Paul Evans, 1970, iron, courtesy Galerie Alexandre Guillemain; *Black Botanica 1* ceramic by Helle Damkjaer, 2019, courtesy of Helle Damkjaer / Galerie Carole Decombe; *Ensemble de trois arbres* ceramic set by Jacques and Dani Ruelland, ca. 1970-80, courtesy of Thomas Fritsch – Artrium © SABAM Belgium, 2021; *Texas* artwork by Ed Ruscha, 1962, oil and printed paper collage on paper, Charles Riva collection © Ed Ruscha. Courtesy of the artist and Gagosian.

Page 59
Automatic Oracle artwork by Robert Motherwell, 1989, acrylic on canvas, Charles Riva collection © Dedalus Foundation / SABAM Belgium, 2021; *Egyptian* stools by Ole Wanscher, 1960, Brazilian rosewood and leather, courtesy New Hope Gallery; desk and chair by Alexandre Noll, ca. 1952, ebony, Daniel Lebard collection © SABAM Belgium, 2021.

Page 61
Black Botanica 1 ceramic by Helle Damkjaer, 2019, courtesy of Helle Damkjaer / Galerie Carole Decombe; cabinet by Paul Evans, 1970, iron, courtesy Galerie Alexandre Guillemain; *Texas* artwork by Ed Ruscha, 1962, oil and printed paper collage on paper, Charles Riva collection © Ed Ruscha. Courtesy of the artist and Gagosian; pot by Mado Jolain, ca. 1960, ceramic, courtesy Galerie Alexandre Guillemain; *Important calice* ceramic by Georges Jouve, ca. 1955, courtesy Galerie Martel Greiner; *Ensemble de trois arbres* ceramics by Jacques and Dani Ruelland, ca. 1970-80, courtesy Thomas Fritsch – Artrium © SABAM Belgium, 2021; desk and chair by Alexandre Noll, ca. 1952, ebony, Daniel Lebard collection © SABAM Belgium, 2021; ceramic by Valérie Hermans, 2012, courtesy the artist and Galerie Arcanes.

Page 62
Bowl by Takuro Kuwata, 2014, porcelain, Olivier Dwek collection, courtesy Pierre Marie Giraud, Brussels.

Page 64
Hanging wall case by Paul Evans, Phillip Lloyd Powell, and George Nakashima, 1964, bronze, copper, gold, silver, walnut, and wicker, courtesy New Hope Gallery; box by Harrison McIntosh, ca. 1960, enameled ceramic, courtesy Galerie Alexandre Guillemain; *Pomme bouche* artwork by Claude Lalanne, 1980, bronze © SABAM Belgium, 2021.

Page 65
Elevational Weights, Vertical Mass artwork by Richard Serra, 2010, Paintstik on paper in artist's frame, Charles Riva collection © SABAM Belgium, 2021; *PK55* table by Poul Kjaerholm, 1957, steel and oak, courtesy New Hope Gallery; *Revolving armchair No. 23* by Charlotte Perriand, 1949, wood © SABAM Belgium, 2021; *Metropole 305 Standard* chairs by Jean Prouvé, 1953, steel and aluminum © SABAM Belgium, 2021; jug by Valentine Schlegel, 1955, terracotta, courtesy Galerie Anne-Sophie Duval © SABAM Belgium, 2021; *Mousse Large Bassin* ceramic by Jean Girel, 2011, courtesy Galerie Arcanes © SABAM Belgium, 2021; mobile by Jacques Jarrige, 2016, aluminum, courtesy Galerie Avant-Scène © SABAM Belgium, 2021.

Pages 66-67
Minguren I coffee table by George Nakashima, ca. 1955, English walnut, courtesy New Hope Gallery; *BO 961* chair by Jørgen Lund and Ole Larsen, 1961, wicker and steel, courtesy New Hope Gallery; *Slab* bench by George Nakashima, ca. 1960, Persian walnut, courtesy New Hope Gallery; *Conoid* room divider by George Nakashima, 1984, cherry-wood, courtesy New Hope Gallery; *Élysée* sofa and armchair by Pierre Paulin, 1972-74, steel, foam and wool; *Contenir le vent "8-VI"* artwork by Brigitte Marionneau, 2019, ceramic, courtesy Galerie Arcanes © Brigitte Marionneau – Modern Shapes Gallery; box by Harrison McIntosh, ca. 1960, ceramic; artwork by Eva Hild, 2009, stoneware, courtesy Mouvements Modernes Gallery © SABAM Belgium, 2021; *Bouteilles épaulées, Roseaux* ceramics by Jacques and Dani Ruelland, 1970, courtesy Thomas Fritsch – Artrium © SABAM Belgium, 2021; *Pomme bouche* artwork by Claude Lalanne, 1980, bronze © SABAM Belgium, 2021; *Untitled* artwork by Christopher Wool, 2016, oil and silkscreen on paper © Christopher Wool. Courtesy of the artist and Luhring Augustine, New York.

Page 69
Soft 2 ceramic by Helle Damkjaer, 2019, courtesy of Helle Damkjaer / Galerie Carole Decombe; *Hibou* artwork by Paul Hanrez, 1995, bronze, courtesy of Paul Hanrez Estate; *Important calice* ceramic by Georges Jouve, ca. 1955, courtesy Galerie Martel Greiner; box by Paul Evans, ca. 1970, resin and bronze, courtesy New Hope Gallery; ceramic bottles by Suzanne Ramié, atelier Madoura, 1952 and 1965, courtesy Thomas Fritsch – Artrium; *Pansue, Figue, Boule Ovoïde,* and *Boule* ceramics by Jacques and Dani Ruelland, 1960, courtesy Thomas Fritsch – Artrium © SABAM Belgium, 2021.

Pages 70-71
Goutte d'eau table by Ado Chale, 1972, bronze, courtesy New Hope Gallery © SABAM Belgium, 2021; vases by Gustavo Pérez, 2005 and 2011, sandstone, courtesy the artist and Galerie Arcanes; *EKC22* chairs by Poul Kjaerholm, 1955, wicker and steel, courtesy New Hope Gallery; *Mousse Large Bassin* ceramic by Jean Girel, 2011, courtesy Galerie Arcanes © SABAM Belgium, 2021; ceramic bottles by Suzanne Ramié, atelier Madoura, 1952 and 1965, courtesy Thomas Fritsch – Artrium; *Pansue, Figue, Boule Ovoïde,* and *Boule* ceramics by Jacques and Dani Ruelland, 1960, courtesy Thomas Fritsch – Artrium © SABAM Belgium, 2021.

CAB Foundation

Page 75
Diagonal Line artwork by Bernar Venet, 2020, steel © SABAM Belgium, 2021.

Pages 76-77
Diagonal Line artwork by Bernar Venet, 2020, steel © SABAM Belgium, 2021; chairs by Jørgen Høj and Poul Kjaerholm, 1951, oak and rope; *Palazzo* low table by Sébastien Caporusso, marble; stools by Stan Bitters, ca. 1960, ceramic, Olivier Dwek collection; vase by Cécile Noguès, 2012, metal and earthenware, Olivier Dwek collection, courtesy Alain Gutharc Gallery.

Pages 78-79
Diagonal Line artwork by Bernar Venet, 2020, steel © SABAM Belgium, 2021; *Diagonal 68.5°* artwork by Bernar Venet, 1979, graphite on wood © SABAM Belgium, 2021.

Edouard Nortier Residence

Page 85
Nuage bookcase by Charlotte Perriand, 1959, aluminum and ash, courtesy Laffanour Galerie Downtown © SABAM Belgium, 2021; *Luge* deck chair by Jean Royère, ca. 1937, steel and goatskin, courtesy Laffanour Galerie Downtown © SABAM Belgium, 2021; stools by Charlotte Perriand, ca. 1950–60, oak, courtesy Laffanour Galerie Downtown © SABAM Belgium, 2021; *Mad Cow* artwork by Christopher Wool, 1997, enamel on aluminum © Christopher Wool. Courtesy of the artist and Luhring Augustine, New York; ceramics by Pol Chambost © SABAM Belgium, 2021; ceramics by Jacques and Dani Ruelland © SABAM Belgium, 2021.

Pages 86-87
Jelly Pea sofa by India Mahdavi, velvet, courtesy Isabelle Reynders; *Arborescence* pedestal table by Eric Robin, iron © SABAM Belgium, 2021; coffee table by Ado Chale, 2012, aluminum, chalcedony agate, and carnelian mosaic, courtesy Studio Ado Chale © SABAM Belgium, 2021; *Minerale* artwork by Ritsue Mishima, 2004, glass, courtesy Pierre Marie Giraud, Brussels; carpet and curtains by Isabelle Reynders; *Committee* chairs by Pierre Jeanneret, ca. 1955, teak and fur, courtesy Laffanour Galerie Downtown; *GH/M 446/1, Heller Quantensprung (John Mauss)* and *GH/M 446/2, Quantensprung (dunkel)* artworks by Gregor Hildebrandt, 2011, cassette tape, dispersion, and adhesive tape on canvas, courtesy of Gregor Hildebrandt and Perrotin; *Chaotic* artwork by Klara Kristalova, 2012, porcelain, courtesy of the artist and Perrotin © SABAM Belgium, 2021; *Composition* ceramic by Louisélio, 2010, courtesy Pierre Marie Giraud, Brussels; *Unknown poet #6* artwork by Hernan Bas, 2012, acrylic, gold leaf, and graphite on gold dusted paper, courtesy of the artist and Perrotin; bench by Mira Nakashima, ca. 2000, wood.

Page 88
Untitled (Z3) artwork by Jannis Kounellis, 1961, tempera on paper, courtesy White Cube Gallery © SABAM Belgium, 2021; *Untitled (Coca Cola)* artwork by Jean-Michel Basquiat, 1982, oil and collage on metal, courtesy Vedovi Gallery © The Estate of Jean-Michel Basquiat / SABAM Belgium, 2021; *Smoker Study #7* artwork by Tom Wesselmann, 1967, oil and graphite on canvas, Charles Riva collection © SABAM Belgium, 2021; *EXHM/DS3* artwork by Sterling Ruby, 2011, collage and paint on cardboard, courtesy the artist and Xavier Hufkens, Brussels; *Collier Gris Mica* artwork by Jean-Michel Othoniel, 2018, Murano glass, courtesy of the artist and Perrotin © SABAM Belgium, 2021; *Or* floor lamp by Eric Robin, iron and gold leaf © SABAM Belgium, 2021; stools by Charlotte Perriand, ca. 1950–60, oak, courtesy Laffanour Galerie Downtown © SABAM Belgium, 2021; *Luge* deck chair by Jean Royère, ca. 1937, steel and goatskin, courtesy Laffanour Galerie Downtown © SABAM Belgium, 2021.

Page 89
Coque wall light by Hervé Van der Straeten, 2004, bronze and brass; *Collier Gris Mica* artwork by Jean-Michel Othoniel, 2018, Murano glass © SABAM Belgium, 2021; chair by Alexandre Noll, ca. 1940, mahogany, courtesy Galerie Jacques Lacoste © SABAM Belgium, 2021.

Page 90
Wall cabinet by George Nakashima, ca. 1969, walnut, courtesy Adam Edelsberg; *Ice Cream Ball* ceramics by Tony Marsh, 2012, courtesy Pierre Marie Giraud, Brussels; *Not There (left and right)* artwork by Louise Lawler, 2003-04, silver dye bleach print, courtesy of the artist and Metro Pictures, New York.

Page 91
GH/M 446/1, Heller Quantensprung (John Mauss) and *GH/M 446/2, Quantensprung (dunkel)* artworks by Gregor Hildebrandt, 2011, cassette tape, dispersion and adhesive tape on canvas, courtesy of Gregor Hildebrandt and Perrotin; chair by Alexandre Noll, ca. 1940, mahogany © SABAM Belgium, 2021; *Not There (left and right)* artwork by Louise Lawler, 2003-04, silver dye bleach print, courtesy of the artist and Metro Pictures, New York; wall cabinet by George Nakashima, ca. 1969, walnut; ceramics by Kristin McKirdy, 2019, courtesy Pierre Marie Giraud, Brussels.

Pages 92-93
Goutte d'eau dining table by Ado Chale, 2010, aluminum courtesy Studio Ado Chale © SABAM Belgium, 2021; *Untitled* artwork by Paola Pivi, 2016, mixed media pearls, courtesy of the artist and Perrotin; ceiling light by Serge Mouille, 1958, metal, aluminum, and brass © SABAM Belgium, 2021; ceramics by Tony Marsh, 2010, courtesy Pierre Marie Giraud, Brussels; *Diagonal Portrait* artwork by George Condo, 2013, acrylic, charcoal, and pastel on canvas, courtesy Simon Lee Gallery © SABAM Belgium, 2021; *Metropole 306 Standard* chairs by Jean Prouvé, 1952, steel and leather, courtesy Laffanour Galerie Downtown © SABAM Belgium, 2021; *Office* chair by Pierre Jeanneret, ca. 1955, teak and wicker, courtesy Laffanour Galerie Downtown; *Leaf* plate by Peter Lane, ceramic, courtesy of the artist and Chahan Gallery.

Page 95
Eye #4 (Roadside Victim) artwork by Alex Prager, 2012, photograph, courtesy Alex Prager Studio and Lehmann Maupin, New York, Hong Kong, Seoul, and London; bowl by John Pawson, bronze.

Page 97
A331 Beehive ceiling lamp by Alvar Aalto, 1953, aluminum and brass; ceramics by Jacques and Dani Ruelland, ca. 1970 © SABAM Belgium, 2021; *Où et Quand ? Nulle Part. Question 6* artwork by Sophie Calle, 2012, calligraphy, photograph under plexiglass, book, handwritten notes, iron frames, book in metal frame,

introductory text, wooden frame, courtesy of the artist and Perrotin © SABAM Belgium, 2021.

Page 98
Ceramics by Tony Marsh, 2010, courtesy Pierre Marie Giraud, Brussels; *Goutte d'eau* dining table by Ado Chale, 2010, aluminum © SABAM Belgium, 2021.

Page 99
Neutra armchairs by Vincent Van Duysen, 2008, aluminum.

Silver House

Pages 114-115
Relief lunaire dining table by Ado Chale, 2012, aluminum, courtesy Studio Ado Chale © SABAM Belgium, 2021; *Arceau* artwork by Ado Chale, ca. 2009, aluminum, courtesy Studio Ado Chale © SABAM Belgium, 2021; bowl by Ado Chale, ca. 2012, aluminum, courtesy Studio Ado Chale © SABAM Belgium, 2021; *Heritage* stacking chairs by Philippe Starck, 2001, aluminum.

Page 119
Harlem Paper artwork by Jean-Michel Basquiat, 1987, acrylic, oil, and paper collage on canvas, courtesy Vedovi Gallery © The Estate of Jean-Michel Basquiat / SABAM Belgium, 2021; folding easy chairs by Johan Hagen, 1958, bentwood, and canvas, courtesy New Hope Gallery; *Barcelona* daybed by Ludwig Mies van der Rohe, 1929, leather, steel, and mahogany © SABAM Belgium, 2021; *Barcelona* coffee table by Ludwig Mies van der Rohe, 1929, glass and steel © SABAM Belgium, 2021.

Etangs d'Ixelles Town House

Page 127
Nothing but Flowers artwork by Thomas Lerooy, 2011, mixed media on paper, courtesy Rodolphe Janssen Gallery © SABAM Belgium, 2021; ceiling light by Serge Mouille, 1958, metal, aluminum, and brass © SABAM Belgium, 2021; *Antony* shelving unit by Jean Prouvé, ca. 1953, steel and oak, courtesy Galerie Patrick Seguin © SABAM Belgium, 2021; ceramics by Jacques and Dani Ruelland, 1970, courtesy Thomas Fritsch – Artrium © SABAM Belgium, 2021; ceramic by Suzanne Ramié, ca. 1950, courtesy Thomas Fritsch – Artrium; *Pyramids and Worlds* artwork by Alexander Calder, 1970, gouache on paper © 2021 Calder Foundation, New York / SABAM Belgium; *Type* chairs by Pierre Jeanneret, ca. 1955, teak and wicker; high stools by Pierre Jeanneret, ca. 1965, teak and cane.

Pages 128-129
PK80 daybed by Poul Kjaerholm, ca. 1950, steel and leather, courtesy New Hope Gallery; *Joséphine* coffee table by Ado Chale, 2013, steel and bronze, courtesy Studio Ado Chale © SABAM Belgium, 2021; *150 BC* sofa by Vladimir Kagan, ca. 1950, maple and wool; *Kangourou* fireside chair by Pierre Jeanneret, ca. 1955, teak and wicker; stools by Charlotte Perriand, ca. 1950–60, oak, courtesy Laffanour Galerie Downtown © SABAM Belgium, 2021; *Committee* chairs by Pierre Jeanneret, ca. 1955, teak and fur, courtesy Laffanour Galerie Downtown; *Bench from Cité Cansado* by Charlotte Perriand, ca. 1958, steel and mahogany © SABAM Belgium, 2021; *Untitled* artwork by Gert and Uwe Tobias, 2005, woodcut on paper, courtesy Rodolphe Janssen Gallery © SABAM Belgium, 2021; ceramic by Takuro Kuwata, 2015, courtesy Pierre Marie Giraud, Brussels; *Infinito* artwork by Ritsue Mishima, 2015, glass, courtesy Pierre Marie Giraud, Brussels ; *Flesh of the Shadow Spirits 60* artwork by Kendell Geers, 2011, resin, courtesy Rodolphe Janssen Gallery © SABAM Belgium, 2021.

Page 131
Untitled artwork by Thomas Houseago, 2015, plaster, hemp, iron, and graphite © SABAM Belgium, 2021; *PK80* daybed by Poul Kjaerholm, ca. 1950, steel and leather; *Committee* chair by Pierre Jeanneret, ca. 1955, teak and fur, courtesy Laffanour Galerie Downtown; *Joséphine* coffee table by Ado Chale, 2013, steel and bronze, courtesy Studio Ado Chale © SABAM Belgium, 2021.

Pages 132-133
Base-building pigeonhole desk by Pierre Jeanneret, ca. 1957, sissoo, aluminum, and leather; *Expansion Bock* artwork by César, 1970, aluminum, courtesy Sorry We're Closed Gallery © SBJ / SABAM Belgium, 2021; *Untitled* artwork by Thomas Houseago, 2015, plaster, hemp, iron rebar, and graphite © SABAM Belgium, 2021; *Louis XXI, porcelaine humaine* artwork by Andrea Branzi, 2010, porcelain, courtesy Mouvements Modernes, Sèvres, Cité de la Céramique © SABAM Belgium, 2021; *Joséphine* coffee table by Ado Chale, 2013, steel and bronze, courtesy Studio Ado Chale © SABAM Belgium, 2021; ceramic by Takuro Kuwata, 2015, courtesy Pierre Marie Giraud, Brussels; *PK80* daybed by Poul Kjaerholm, ca. 1950, steel and leather; *Office* chair by Pierre Jeanneret, ca. 1955, teak and wicker, courtesy Laffanour Galerie Downtown; *Kangourou* fireside chair by Pierre Jeanneret, ca. 1955, teak and wicker; *Committee* chairs by Pierre Jeanneret, ca. 1955, teak and fur.

Page 134
Expansion Bock artwork by César, 1970, aluminum, courtesy Sorry We're Closed Gallery © SBJ / SABAM Belgium, 2021; *Louis XXI, porcelaine humaine* artwork by Andrea Branzi, 2010, porcelain, courtesy Mouvements Modernes, Sèvres, Cité de la Céramique © SABAM Belgium, 2021; *Pink Clown* artwork from PROPO series by Paul McCarthy, 1991 (2008), cibachrome mounted on aluminum, courtesy the artist and Xavier Hufkens, Brussels.

Page 137
BC (4384) artwork by Sterling Ruby, 2013, collage, paint, bleach, glue, and fabric on wood, courtesy the artist and Xavier Hufkens, Brussels; *Plug* table by Rick Owens, plywood, courtesy Pierre Marie Giraud, Brussels; *Type* chairs by Pierre Jeanneret, ca. 1955, teak and wicker, courtesy Laffanour Galerie Downtown; *Metropole 306 Standard* chairs by Jean Prouvé, 1952, steel and leather courtesy Laffanour Galerie Downtown © SABAM Belgium, 2021; ceramic by Akiyama Yo, 2014, courtesy Pierre Marie Giraud, Brussels.

Pages 138-139
Bench by Pierre Jeanneret, ca. 1955, teak and cane, courtesy Laffanour Galerie Downtown.

N.E.S.T. Foundation

Page 143
Untitled artwork by Danh Vo, 2016, gold, and ink on cardboard, courtesy of the artist and Galerie Chantal Crousel, Paris; *We the People (detail)* artwork by Danh Vo, 2011-16, copper, courtesy of the artist and Galerie Chantal Crousel, Paris; *Paper Drop (passage) VI* artwork by Wolfgang Tillmans, 2019, inkjet print on paper, image by Wolfgang Tillmans.

Pages 144-145
Untitled artwork by Danh Vo, 2016, gold and ink on cardboard, courtesy of the artist and Galerie Chantal Crousel, Paris; *We the People (detail)* artworks by Danh Vo, 2011-16, copper, courtesy of the artist and Galerie Chantal Crousel, Paris; *Paper Drop (passage) VI* artwork by Wolfgang Tillmans, 2019, inkjet print on paper, image by Wolfgang Tillmans; *No-Rat Box* artwork by Danh Vo, 2010, gold leaf on cardboard, courtesy of the artist and Galerie Chantal Crousel, Paris.

Page 147
Untitled (F52) artwork by Christopher Wool, 1992, alkyd and pencil on card © Christopher Wool. Courtesy of the artist and Luhring Augustine, New York; *Refuse* artwork by Gavin Turk, 2012, bronze, Copyright The Artist, Courtesy Live Stock Market Ltd & Gavin Turk; *And I Trust You* artwork by Tracey Emin, 2015, neon © Tracey Emin. All rights reserved, SABAM Belgium, 2021.

Page 148
Anthropomorphe floor lamp by Philippe Hiquily, 1993, resin, courtesy Galerie Yves Gastou © SABAM Belgium, 2021; *Untitled ("Club" Fauteuil)* armchair by Franz West, 2015, steel, wood, foam, and linen © Archiv Franz West © Estate Franz West; *Cloud* coffee table by Jacques Hervouet, oak; *Poisson* dish by Séraphin Soudbinine, courtesy Galerie Anne-Sophie Duval; *Waiting for Godot 296157-296941* and *Waiting for Godot 100099-101696* ceramics by Sejin Bae, 2019, courtesy Mouvements Modernes Gallery; ceramics by Kristin McKirdy, 2018, courtesy Pierre Marie Giraud, Brussels; *On the Rocks* sofa by Francesco Binfare, 2004, upholstery, courtesy InStore; *Silence is Golden / Talk or Die* artwork by Bruce Nauman, 1983, neon © SABAM Belgium, 2021; *Geiler Gaul* artwork by Franz West, 2005, papier-mâché, styropor, steel, acrylic, and enamel © Archiv Franz West © Estate Franz West; *Bagatelle* artwork by Franz West, 1982, dispersion, oil, papier-mâché, plaster © Archiv Franz West © Estate Franz West; *Partial Truth* artwork by Bruce Nauman, 1997, silkscreen on paper © SABAM Belgium, 2021.

Page 149
Untitled artwork by Günther Förg, 2007, acrylic and oil on canvas, © Estate Günther Förg, Suisse / VG Bild-Kunst, Bonn 2021.

Pages 150-151
Untitled ("Club" Fauteuil) armchairs by Franz West, 2015, steel, wood, foam, and linen © Archiv Franz West © Estate Franz West; divan by Franz West, 1998, steel, wood, foam, and linen © Archiv Franz West © Estate Franz West; *Cloud* table by Jacques Hervouet, oak; *Plat poisson* by Séraphin Soudbinine, courtesy Galerie Anne-Sophie Duval; *Waiting for Godot 296157-296941* and *Waiting for Godot 100099-101696* ceramics by Sejin Bae, 2019, courtesy Mouvements Modernes Gallery; ceramics by Kristin McKirdy, 2018, courtesy Pierre Marie Giraud, Brussels; *On The Rocks* sofa by Francesco Binfare, 2004, upholstery, courtesy InStore; *Anthropomorphe* floor lamp by Philippe Hiquily, 1993, resin, courtesy Galerie Yves Gastou © SABAM Belgium, 2021; *Untitled* artwork by Christopher Wool, 1998, enamel on canvas © Christopher Wool. Courtesy of the artist and Luhring Augustine, New York; *Studies for Holograms (a-e)* artworks by Bruce Nauman, 1970, screen prints on paper © SABAM Belgium, 2021.

Page 152
Untitled ("Club" Fauteuil) armchair by Franz West, 2015, steel, wood, foam, and linen © Archiv Franz West © Estate Franz West; divan by Franz West, 1998, steel, wood, foam, and linen © Archiv Franz West © Estate Franz West; *Cloud* table by Jacques Hervouet, oak; *Waiting for Godot 100099-101696* ceramic by Sejin Bae, 2019, courtesy Mouvements Modernes Gallery; *S.A.M TS 11* table by Jean Prouvé, ca. 1942, wood and steel © SABAM Belgium, 2021; *Tout bois* chairs by Jean Prouvé, 1953, wood and plywood © SABAM Belgium, 2021; *Large Swan, Small Shell* and *Large Flower* vases by Malene Knudsen, 2020, ceramic, courtesy Malene Knudsen and BOON_ROOM Gallery, 9 rue de lesdiguières, Paris IV; *Codex Monotypes #30* artwork by Julie Mehretu, 2018, ink and acrylic on paper © Julie Mehretu. Courtesy White Cube and Marian Goodman Gallery; *Painting for T.* artwork by Secundino Hernández, 2017, acrylic and medium on canvas © SABAM Belgium, 2021.

Page 153
Nature's Privy Seal artwork by Jason Rhoades, 2003, neon and plexiglass © The Estate of Jason Rhoades.

Page 154
Bar by Olivier Dwek, 2019, tin; *MT 344* stool by Pierre Chareau, 1926, steel and wood; pendant by Jules Wabbes, nickel-plated brass, 1968.

Page 155
Table by Arne Jacobsen, 1956-58, aluminum and wenge; *PK9* chairs by Poul Kjaerholm, ca. 1961, stainless steel and leather, courtesy New Hope

Gallery; *Totem* candleholders by Franck Evennou, bronze, courtesy Avant-Scène © SABAM Belgium, 2021; *Large Blue Starfish* vase by Antoinette Faragallah, courtesy of the artist and Chahan Gallery; golden cups by Shizue Imai, courtesy of the artist and Chahan Gallery; spherical candleholder by Pierre Forssell, 1967, brass, courtesy Jimmy Beyens Gallery; *Crown* candleholder by Pierre Forssell, 1978, brass, courtesy Jimmy Beyens Gallery; adjustable candleholder by Pierre Forssell, 1969, brass, courtesy Jimmy Beyens Gallery; *Crescent* candleholders by Pierre Forssell, 1969, brass, courtesy Jimmy Beyens Gallery; *Propeller* candleholder by Pierre Forssell, 1978, brass, courtesy Jimmy Beyens Gallery; candleholders by Pierre Forssell, 1978, brass, courtesy Jimmy Beyens Gallery; trio set candleholder by Pierre Forssell, 1975, brass, courtesy Jimmy Beyens Gallery; bar by Olivier Dwek, 2019, hammered tin; *MT 344* stools by Pierre Chareau, 1926, steel and wood; pendants by Jules Wabbes, nickel-plated brass, 1968.

Page 157
Arbeitstisch in Aspik table by Franz West, 2008, wood, acrylic, lacquer, resin and steel © Archiv Franz West © Estate Franz West; *Tout bois* chair by Jean Prouvé, 1953, wood and plywood, courtesy Galerie Patrick Seguin © SABAM Belgium, 2021; *Boule, Bilobé, Ovoïde*, and *Balustre* vases by Louis Lourioux, courtesy Galerie Arcanes; *The Drawers and I* desk by Martin Szekely, 2018, wood and brass, courtesy Pierre Marie Giraud, Brussels; *Soft Pad* chair by Charles and Ray Eames, ca. 1950, aluminum and leather; table lamp by George Nakashima, 1973, American walnut and holly, courtesy Alexandre Guillemain; boxes by Alexandre Noll, ca. 1950, ebony, courtesy Galerie Jacques Lacoste © SABAM Belgium, 2021; trilobe vase by Henri Simmen, courtesy Galerie Anne-Sophie Duval; two-handle vase by Henri Simmen, courtesy Galerie Anne-Sophie Duval.

Page 158
The Drawers and I desk by Martin Szekely, 2018, wood and brass, courtesy Pierre Marie Giraud, Brussels; *Soft Pad* chair by Charles and Ray Eames, ca. 1950, aluminum and leather; table lamp by George Nakashima, 1973, American walnut and holly, courtesy Alexandre Guillemain; boxes by Alexandre Noll, ca. 1950, ebony, courtesy Galerie Jacques Lacoste © SABAM Belgium, 2021; trilobe vase by Henri Simmen, courtesy Galerie Anne-Sophie Duval; two-handle vase by Henri Simmen, courtesy Galerie Anne-Sophie Duval.

Page 161
Camaleonda modular sofa by Mario Bellini, 1970, upholstery, courtesy InStore; *Ox* chairs by Hans Wegner, 1960, steel and upholstery; *Aztèque* coffee tables by Agnès Debizet, 2020, sandstone and porcelain, courtesy Galerie Yves Gastou; *1089* vase by Pol Chambost, 1955, ceramic, courtesy Thomas Fritsch – Artrium © SABAM Belgium, 2021; *Pansu* vase by Georges Jouve, 1956, ceramic, courtesy Thomas Fritsch – Artrium; *Boule aplatie* vase by Georges Jouve, 1957, ceramic, courtesy Thomas Fritsch – Artrium; *Patte d'ours* ashtray by Georges Jouve, 1951, ceramic, courtesy Thomas Fritsch – Artrium.

Pages 162-163
Low table by André Aleth Masson, 1962, ceramic and metal, courtesy Thomas Fritsch – Artrium © SABAM Belgium, 2021; Ox chairs by Hans Wegner, 1960, steel and upholstery; *Camaleonda* modular sofa by Mario Bellini, 1970, fabric or leather upholstery, courtesy InStore; *Aztèque* coffee tables by Agnès Debizet, 2020, sandstone and porcelain, courtesy Galerie Yves Gastou; *1089* vase by Pol Chambost, 1955, ceramic, courtesy Thomas Fritsch – Artrium © SABAM Belgium, 2021; *Pansu* vase by Georges Jouve, 1956, ceramic, courtesy Thomas Fritsch – Artrium; *Boule aplatie* vase by Georges Jouve, 1957, ceramic, courtesy Thomas Fritsch – Artrium; *Patte d'ours* ashtray by Georges Jouve, 1951, ceramic, courtesy Thomas Fritsch – Artrium; *Nénuphar* floor lamp by Philippe Hiquily, 1985, aluminum, courtesy Galerie Yves Gastou © SABAM Belgium, 2021; *The Algiers' Sections of a Happy Moment* artwork by David Claerbout, 2010, photograph © David Claerbout; *Matterhorn* artwork by Kris Martin, 2009, print, courtesy of the artist and KÖNIG GALERIE Berlin, London; *Trompette* floor lamp by Pierre Paulin, ca. 1970, metal, courtesy Jousse Entreprise; 2001: *Metropolis*, film by Fritz Lang, 1927.

Les Mélèzes Town House

Page 167
Office chair by Pierre Jeanneret, ca. 1955, teak and wicker, courtesy Laffanour Galerie Downtown; *Reclining Figure* artwork by Thomas Houseago, 2008, aluminum, Olivier Dwek collection, courtesy the Artist and Xavier Hufkens © SABAM Belgium, 2021.

Page 168
Poire ceramic by Georges Jouve, ca. 1955, courtesy Laffanour Galerie Downtown.

Page 169
High Court Down sofa by Pierre Jeanneret, ca. 1955, teak and foalskin, courtesy Laffanour Galerie Downtown; *Slab* coffee table by George Nakashima, 1963, American walnut, courtesy New Hope Gallery; ceramic by Georges Jouve, ca. 1945, courtesy Laffanour Galerie Downtown; *Poire* ceramic by Georges Jouve, ca. 1955, courtesy Laffanour Galerie Downtown; daybed by Charlotte Perriand, ca. 1956-1959, courtesy Laffanour Galerie Downtown © SABAM Belgium, 2021; *Untitled* artwork by Jacob Kassay, 2012, acrylic and silver deposit on canvas, courtesy the artist and Art: Concept, Paris.

Page 170
Untitled (Placebo) installation by Simon Nicaise, 2010, courtesy Bodson-Emelinckx Gallery © SABAM Belgium, 2021.

Page 171
Ombre chair by Charlotte Perriand, 1958, plywood, courtesy Laffanour Galerie Downtown © SABAM Belgium, 2021; *Untitled (Placebo)* installation by Simon Nicaise, 2010, courtesy Bodson-Emelinckx Gallery © SABAM Belgium, 2021.

Pages 172-173
Bridge Director armchair by Jean Prouvé, ca. 1950, leather, oak, and steel © SABAM Belgium, 2021, courtesy Laffanour Galerie Downtown; desk by Pierre Jeanneret, ca. 1955, teak, courtesy Laffanour Galerie Downtown; *SP230* artwork by Sterling Ruby, 2013, spray paint on canvas, courtesy the Artist and Xavier Hufkens, Brussels.

Page 174
Ceramic by Georges Jouve, ca. 1945, courtesy Laffanour Galerie Downtown.

Page 175
Reclining Figure artwork by Thomas Houseago, 2008, aluminum, Olivier Dwek collection, courtesy the Artist and Xavier Hufkens © SABAM Belgium, 2021; *Office* chair by Pierre Jeanneret, ca. 1955, teak and wicker, courtesy Laffanour Galerie Downtown; bookcase by Olivier Dwek, 2008, larch wood; Keaka statue, Cameroon or Nigeria, wood and animal hide, courtesy Didier Claes; Dogon Walu mask, Mali, wood, courtesy Didier Claes; "white" mask, Fang or Okande, Gabon, courtesy Didier Claes; *Transcompositional/Fur + tattoo* artwork by Sterling Ruby, 2009, nail polish and collage on mirror paper, courtesy the artist and Xavier Hufkens, Brussels; stools by Charlotte Perriand, ca. 1950–60, oak, courtesy Laffanour Galerie Downtown © SABAM Belgium, 2021.

Page 177
Table by Charlotte Perriand, 1949, pine, courtesy Laffanour Galerie Downtown © SABAM Belgium, 2021; stools by Charlotte Perriand, ca. 1950–60, oak, courtesy Laffanour Galerie Downtown © SABAM Belgium, 2021; *Untitled (P 583)* artwork by Christopher Wool, 2009, silkscreen ink on linen mounted on aluminum © Christopher Wool. Courtesy of the artist and Luhring Augustine, New York.

Page 178
Stools by Charlotte Perriand, ca. 1950–60, oak, courtesy Laffanour Galerie Downtown © SABAM Belgium, 2021.

Page 179
Bridge Director armchair by Jean Prouvé, ca. 1950, leather, oak, and steel, courtesy Laffanour Galerie Downtown © SABAM Belgium, 2021; desk by Pierre Jeanneret, ca. 1955, teak.

Page 180
Afterimage 09-330 artwork by Byung Hoon Choï, 2009, marble and stone, courtesy Laffanour Galerie Downtown.

Seaflower Residence

Page 185
It Doesn't Matter My Friend, It Does Not Matter, To Cry Is Beautiful artwork by Tracey Emin, 2004, neon © Tracey Emin. All rights reserved, SABAM Belgium, 2021; *Ninth Copper Cardinal* artwork by Carl Andre, 1973, copper plates © SABAM Belgium, 2021; *Stag* stool by Rick Owens, 2015, elm and moose antler, courtesy Pierre Marie Giraud, Brussels.

Page 186
East Indian Laurel Frenchmans Cove table by George Nakashima, laurel; chair by Alexandre Noll, ca. 1940, mahogany, courtesy Galerie Jacques Lacoste © SABAM Belgium, 2021; *Library* chairs by Pierre Jeanneret, ca. 1960, teak and wicker; *Hekiyu Renmonki* ceramic by Yoshiro Kimura, 2015, courtesy Pierre Marie Giraud, Brussels; *Double Large Figures* artwork by Juan Muñoz, 1991, bronze © Juan Muñoz Estate / SABAM Belgium 2021; *Untitled* artwork by Secundino Hernández, 2016, glue, chalk, calcium carbonate, and titanium white on canvas © SABAM Belgium, 2021.

Page 187
Double Large Figures artwork by Juan Muñoz, 1991, bronze © Juan Muñoz Estate / SABAM Belgium 2021; *Untitled* artwork by Secundino Hernández, 2016, glue, chalk, calcium carbonate, and titanium white on canvas © SABAM Belgium, 2021.

Page 188
Flaque coffee table by Jean Royère, ca. 1952, straw marquetry, courtesy Laffanour Galerie Downtown © SABAM Belgium, 2021; two openings vase and *Cratère* vase by Georges Jouve, 1950 and 1957, ceramic, courtesy Thomas Fritsch – Artrium; *En Peau* armchair by Charlotte Perriand, 1946, wood and cowskin, courtesy Laffanour Galerie Downtown © SABAM Belgium, 2021; *Untitled* artwork by Jean-Michel Basquiat, 1981, oil on paper © The Estate of Jean-Michel Basquiat / SABAM Belgium, 2021.

Page 189
East Indian Laurel Frenchmans Cove table by George Nakashima, laurel; chair by Alexandre Noll, ca. 1940, mahogany, courtesy Galerie Jacques Lacoste © SABAM Belgium, 2021; *Tokyo* bench by Charlotte Perriand, ca. 1950, ash, courtesy Galerie Jacques Lacoste © SABAM Belgium, 2021; ceramic by Kristin McKirdy, 2016 © Kristin McKirdy/Galerie Jousse entreprise; *Untitled* "stack" artwork by Donald Judd, 1965, iron © Judd Foundation/SABAM Belgium, 2021.

Pages 190-191
Ours polaire sofa and armchair by Jean Royère, ca. 1950, wood and fabric, courtesy Galerie Patrick Seguin and Galerie Jacques Lacoste © SABAM Belgium, 2021; carpet by Olivier Dwek, 2016, silk; stool by Charlotte Perriand, ca. 1950–60, oak © SABAM Belgium, 2021; *En Peau* armchair by Charlotte Perriand, 1946, wood and cowskin, courtesy Laffanour Galerie Downtown © SABAM Belgium, 2021; *Flaque* coffee table by Jean Royère, ca. 1952, straw marquetry, courtesy Laffanour Galerie Downtown © SABAM Belgium, 2021; two openings vase and

Cratère vase by Georges Jouve, 1950 and 1957, ceramic, courtesy Thomas Fritsch – Artrium; *Warthog* floor lamp by Richard Texier, 2019, bronze, courtesy Laffanour Galerie Downtown © SABAM Belgium, 2021; chairs by Alexandre Noll, ca. 1940, mahogany, courtesy Galerie Jacques Lacoste © SABAM Belgium, 2021; *Library* chair by Pierre Jeanneret, ca. 1960, teak and wicker; *East Indian Laurel Frenchmans Cove* table by George Nakashima, laurel; *Hekiyu Renmonki* ceramic by Yoshiro Kimura, 2015, courtesy Pierre Marie Giraud, Brussels; *Double Large Figures* artwork by Juan Muñoz, 1991, bronze © Juan Muñoz Estate / SABAM Belgium 2021; *Untitled* artwork by Secundino Hernández, 2016, glue, chalk, calcium carbonate, and titanium white on canvas © SABAM Belgium, 2021; *La Liberté de l'esprit* artwork by René Magritte, 1949, graphite on paper © Succession René Magritte – SABAM Belgium 2021; *Cavalier et cheval* pitcher by Pablo Picasso, 1952, terracotta and earthenware © Succession Picasso – SABAM Belgium 2021; *Péril extra jaune* artwork by James Ensor, 1938, oil on panel; Lega mask, Congo Basin, early 20th century, wood, courtesy Didier Claes Gallery.

Page 193

Carpet by Olivier Dwek, 2016, silk; stools by Charlotte Perriand, ca. 1950–60, oak, courtesy Laffanour Galerie Downtown © SABAM Belgium, 2021; *Forme libre* table by Charlotte Perriand, 1967, mahogany, courtesy Laffanour Galerie Downtown © SABAM Belgium, 2021; *Bridge Director* armchair by Jean Prouvé, ca. 1950, steel, skai, and wood, courtesy Laffanour Galerie Downtown © SABAM Belgium, 2021; *Tea bowl* ceramic by Takuro Kuwata, 2016, courtesy Pierre Marie Giraud, Brussels; *Cadeau* artwork by Man Ray, 1921-70, iron and nails © Man Ray 2015 Trust / Sabam Belgium 2021; *Quintet* artwork by Berend Strik, 2002, mixed media embroidery on canvas © SABAM Belgium, 2021; *Untitled* artwork by Dan Van Severen, 1979, tempera on tempera cloth on panel © SABAM Belgium, 2021; *Untitled* artwork by Wolfgang Laib, 2001, crayon and pencil © Wolfgang Laib; *Leaping Hare (facing right)* artwork by Barry Flanagan, 1996, inkjet print © The Estate of Barry Flanagan. Courtesy Plubronze Limited, 2021; *De Gendarmen* artwork by James Ensor, 1888, etching on simili paper; *Fourmi* and *Petite Voile* ceramics by Georges Jouve, ca. 1950 and 1957, ceramic, and steel, courtesy Matthieu Richard Galerie; *Swing-Jib* lamp by Jean Prouvé, 1957, steel tube, wire, and sheet, courtesy Galerie Patrick Seguin © SABAM Belgium, 2021; *Figue* vase by Georges Jouve, ca. 1950, sandstone, courtesy Mathieu Richard; *Banane* bowl by Georges Jouve, ca. 1955, sandstone; *Untitled* photograph by Ludwig Vandevelde, 1987; *Monument for the Romantic Poet (Oscar Wilde)* artwork by Barry Flanagan, 1990, pencil on paper © The Estate of Barry Flanagan. Courtesy Plubronze Limited, 2021; *We The People (detail)* artwork by Danh Vo, 2011-2016, copper, courtesy of the artist and Galerie Chantal Crousel, Paris; Dan masks, Ivory Coast, wood, courtesy Yann Ferrandin Galerie; Kota Reliquary Statues, Gabon, late 19th century–early 20th century, wood, copper, and brass, courtesy Didier Claes Gallery.

Page 194

Ours polaire sofa and armchair by Jean Royère, ca. 1950, wood, and fabric, courtesy Galerie Patrick Seguin and Galerie Jacques Lacoste © SABAM Belgium, 2021; carpet by Olivier Dwek, 2016, silk; stools by Charlotte Perriand, ca. 1950–60, oak, courtesy Laffanour Galerie Downtown © SABAM Belgium, 2021; *Forme libre* table by Charlotte Perriand, 1967, mahogany, courtesy Laffanour Galerie Downtown © SABAM Belgium, 2021; tea bowl by Takuro Kuwata, 2016, porcelain, glaze, platinum, palladium, stainless, epoxy resin, and lacquer, courtesy Pierre Marie Giraud, Brussels; *Lapis* artwork by Terry Winters, 2014, oil, wax, and alkyd on linen © Terry Winters, courtesy Matthew Marks Gallery.

Page 196

MAR.11,1990 artwork by On Kawara, 1990, acrylic on canvas © One Million Years Foundation; *Bagatelle* artwork by Franz West, 1982, dispersion, oil, papier-mâché, plaster © Archiv Franz West © Estate Franz West.

Page 197

High stools by Pierre Jeanneret, ca. 1965, teak and cane; *B* candlestick by Richard Texier, 2009, bronze, courtesy Laffanour Galerie Downtown © SABAM Belgium, 2021; *Cornet* vase and *Coq* pitcher vase by Roger Capron, 1955 and 1956, ceramic, courtesy Galerie Thomas Fritsch – Artrium © SABAM Belgium, 2021; *Zen Print #1* and *Zen Print #2* artworks by Brice Marden, 2010, woodcut on paper © SABAM Belgium, 2021.

Page 199

Jackie artwork by Andy Warhol, 1964, acrylic and silkscreen on canvas © The Andy Warhol Foundation for the Visual Arts, Inc./SABAM Belgium 2021.

Pages 200-201

Mocho stool by Sergio Rodrigues, ca. 1960, rosewood; *Imagine* artwork by Tracey Emin, 2007, monoprint © Tracey Emin. All rights reserved, SABAM Belgium, 2021; *Yes* artwork by Tracey Emin, 2007, monoprint © Tracey Emin. All rights reserved, SABAM Belgium, 2021; *The Prophet* artwork by Francis Alÿs, 2001, oil and encaustic on canvas © Francis Alÿs; *No Title (The Place, The ...)* artwork by Raymond Pettibon, 1992, pen and ink on paper © Raymond Pettibon; *No Title (What Was Before)* artwork by Raymond Pettibon, 2002, pen and ink on paper © Raymond Pettibon; *Untitled (WMD, no. 4D)* artwork by Robert Longo, 2007, graphite on paper © SABAM Belgium, 2021; *The Angel* artwork by Michaël Borremans, 2014, etching on paper © Michaël Borremans; *Coming on the Floor* artwork by Tracey Emin, 2007, monoprint © Tracey Emin. All rights reserved, SABAM Belgium, 2021; *Never Again* artwork by Tracey Emin, 2007, monoprint © Tracey Emin. All rights reserved, SABAM Belgium, 2021; *No Title (To the Owner...)* artwork by Raymond Pettibon, 2003, pen and ink on paper © Raymond Pettibon; *Untitled* artworks by Francis Alÿs, 2004, painted photograph © Francis Alÿs; *Deux couleurs* artwork by Willem Cole, 2006, print on paper; *Nicht Hier 1* artwork by Wolfgang Laib, 1996, pencil and pastel on paper © Wolfgang Laib; *Map no. 39* artwork by Tom Molloy, 2006, collage on US dollar bill, courtesy the artist and Lora Reynolds Gallery; floor lamp by Richard Texier, 2019, bronze, courtesy Laffanour Galerie Downtown © SABAM Belgium, 2021.

Page 202

Double Poke in the Eye II artwork by Bruce Nauman, 1985, neon © SABAM Belgium, 2021.

Page 203

Untitled artwork by Rudolf Stingel, 1989, oil and enamel on canvas, 110 1/4 x 70 7/8 in (280 x 180 cm). © Rudolf Stingel. Courtesy Paula Cooper Gallery, New York; *1 2 3 4 5 4 3 2 1* artwork by Sol LeWitt, 1987, aluminum © SABAM Belgium, 2021.

Page 205

Tout bois chair by Jean Prouvé, 1953, wood and plywood, courtesy Galerie Patrick Seguin © SABAM Belgium, 2021; *S.A.M TS 11* table, Jean Prouvé, ca. 1942, wood and steel, courtesy Galerie Patrick Seguin © SABAM Belgium, 2021; *Waterways* artwork by Ritsue Mishima, 2017, glass, courtesy Pierre Marie Giraud, Brussels; *Amor Fati Leaning* artwork by Sterling Ruby, 2017, ceramic, courtesy the Artist and Xavier Hufkens, Brussels *Untitled* artwork by Günther Förg, 1989, acrylic and lead on wooden panel, courtesy Patrick De Brock Gallery © Estate Günther Förg, Suisse / VG Bild-Kunst, Bonn 2021; *Weed* artwork by Tony Matelli, 2007, bronze and paint, courtesy Tony Matelli and Andréhn-Schiptjenko Stockholm Paris; *Stag* stool by Rick Owens, 2015, elm wood, moose antler, courtesy Pierre Marie Giraud, Brussels.

Pages 206-207

Stools by Charlotte Perriand, ca. 1950–60, oak, courtesy Laffanour Galerie Downtown © SABAM Belgium, 2021; *DC1902* coffee table by Vincenzo De Cotiis, 2019, aluminum, Murano glass, brass, and silvered glass, courtesy Carpenters Workshop Gallery; *Reishaus* artwork by Wolfgang Laib, 2002, marble, rice and pollen © Wolfgang Laib; *Tea Bowl* ceramic by Takuro Kuwata, 2018, courtesy Pierre Marie Giraud, Brussels; bowl by Takuro Kuwata, 2014, porcelain, courtesy Pierre Marie Giraud, Brussels; Nkondi Kongo-Vili Fetiche statue, Congo Basin, early 20th century, wood, pigments, vegetal fibers, metal, and glass, courtesy Didier Claes Gallery; sofa by René Drouet, ca. 1950, beech and velvet, courtesy Galerie Jacques Lacoste; floor lamp by Georges Jouve, ca. 1955, ceramic and brass, courtesy Galerie Jacques Lacoste; *Kangourou* fireside chair by Pierre Jeanneret, ca. 1955, teak and wicker.

Olivier Dwek in the light of modernity

First published in the United States of America in 2021
by Rizzoli International Publications, Inc.
300 Park Avenue South – New York, NY 10010
www.rizzoliusa.com

Text: Philip Jodidio

Photographs:
Philippe Garcia: cover and pages 22, 51-71, 75-81, 143-163, 185-207
Serge Anton: pages 11, 12, 14, 15, 105-123, 167-181
Jarmo Pohjaniemi: pages 9, 27-47
Jérôme Galland: pages 85, 88-93, 96-101
Belén Imaz: pages 127-139
Jean-François Jaussaud: pages 18-19, 21, 86-87, 95

Publisher: Charles Miers
Editorial Director: Catherine Bonifassi
Editor: Victorine Lamothe
Production Director: Maria Pia Gramaglia
Managing Editor: Lynn Scrabis

Artistic Direction: Cakedesign
Thibaut Mathieu, Camille Favier

Editorial Coordination: Cassi Edition
Vanessa Blondel, Lili Doillon, Chloé Batallan,
Claire Chamot, Harriet Graham

ISBN: 978-0-8478-6845-2
Library of Congress Control Number: 2020934925
2021 2022 2023 2024 / 10 9 8 7 6 5 4 3 2 1
Printed in Italy

Visit us online:
Facebook.com/RizzoliNewYork
Twitter: @Rizzoli_Books
Instagram.com/RizzoliBooks
Pinterest.com/RizzoliBooks
Youtube.com/RizzoliNY
Issuu.com/Rizzoli